Hearth and Field

FIELDSTONE HEARTH

Hearth and Field
A Heathen Prayer Book
2nd Edition

Hester Butler-Ehle

FIELDSTONE HEARTH

ISBN 978-1-105-74186-9
Second edition. Copyright (c) 2010, 2011 by Hester Butler-Ehle. All rights reserved. No part
of this book may be reproduced without the permission of the author.
Published by Fieldstone Hearth.
Printed by Lulu in the United States of America http://www.lulu.com/
Cover image includes blot-bowl by Karl Donaldsson and hammer by Mark Stinson

For Winterhof,
as always.

Contents

Rituals

Introduction to the 2nd Edition

This is a book that was unintended.

By that I mean that I did not intend to write a book. My intention was to write prayers and rituals to honor the gods, for my own use and for that of Winterhof, my kindred. The first edition of this book came about because I had a fair amount of material and was tired of keeping track of it as bits and pieces. I thought a bound book would make it easier to find things when I needed them, and in fact it did—mission accomplished.

However, when I used it, I was surprised (and perhaps a little embarrassed) by my kindred members' prodding to make my book of prayers available so they could get a copy of their own.

And when I wrote more (because there is no end to these things, as anyone who writes for the gods will attest), they encouraged me to put out another edition. So I did, and this is it.

Nearly double the size of its predecessor, this editions adds not only many new prayers, but also a collection of rituals and a table of contents.

Therefore I'd like to thank the people who did the encouraging—my kindred sisters and brothers, the members of Winterhof. Not just for the encouragement but for everything. I'd also like to thank my husband, Dan, who took on the role of editor—and whom you can thank for the fact that there is a table of contents to refer to in finding your way around the book.

—Hester Butler-Ehle
January 2012

Prayer Book

A Daily Devotion

Hail to Odin, ruthless seeker of wisdom,
far-seeing persuader, bender of what will be.

Hail to Frigga, exacting mistress of the home,
seeress and spinner whose gifts weave through our lives.

Hail to Thor, strong-armed defender of Midgard,
red-bearded rain-bringer, faithful friend of mankind.

Hail to Sif, golden-haired goddess, dear wife of Thor,
treasure of the gods, bringer of life to the cold earth.

Hail to Frey, giver of wealth of gold and grain alike,
of peace and protection, of joy and of pleasure.

Hail to Freya, who stirs sweet desire and keen-edged strife,
seeress, sorceress, strong-willed holder of war-dead.

Hail to Tyr, one-armed granter of justice deserved,
Thing-warder, wolf-binder, strong-minded foe of chaos.

Hail to Skadhi, sharp-minded huntress, winter's maid,
bow-woman, vengeance-seeker, shining bride of Njord.

Hail to Ullr, snowshoe god, friend of hunters,
unsurpassed, glory of the gods.

Hail to Eir, soft-handed healer, gentle goddess
whose touch brings relief from ills of all kinds.

Hail to Heimdall, constant guardian of bright Bifrost,
keen-eyed giver of clear thought, father of men.

Hail to Nerthus, ancient and unfathomable,
holder of the black earth and of the seeds within.

Hail to Njord, fair-footed husband of fierce Skadhi,
friend of sailors, seacoast-dweller, giver of wealth.

Hail to Bragi, foremost of skalds, rune-tongued master
of inspiration's fire, of wordcraft's labor.

Hail to Idunna, keeper of the treasured fruit
of youth and vigor, radiant renewer of life.

Hail to Forseti, law-giver and law-keeper,
arbiter, peacemaker, mender of fences.

Hail to Hella, host of our beloved dead,
inevitable one to whom we all will go

Hail to Aegir, best of brewers, best of hosts,
master of the dark sea depths and all they hold.

Hail to Ran, ocean-queen, keeper of Aegir's hall,
stirrer of storms, both bane and reprieve of ships at sea.

Hail to Balder, brightest son of farseeing Odin,
final hope of the gods, final hope of all the worlds.

Hail to Nanna, bold-hearted bride of Balder,
strong one, true one, holding fast to hearth and heart.

Hail to Jord, deep-souled mother of red-bearded Thor,
enduring holder of breath and blood, sea and stone.

Aegir

master of the dark sea depths

Hail to Aegir, master of the dark sea depths,
father of the nine daughters, companion of Ran,
brewer of the finest ale, maker of sweet mead,
most generous of hosts, we honor you this day.
Here we stand each year, gathered together,
long journeys behind us, longer still ahead,
to meet with friends old and new, to share food and drink,
to reminisce and to make new memories,
to blot and to sumbel, to greet the gods together,
at this time, in this place, with these folk. Hail Aegir!

Aegir

a welcoming horn of mead

Hail to Aegir, best of brewers, best of hosts!
Deep-dwelling husband of fearsome, beautiful Ran;
father of the nine daughters, nine fair maids whose dance
and play set ships to roll upon the sea. Aegir,
your generosity and openheartedness
are known to all, your great and spacious hall
often filled with fond friends, with noble company.
We know you in fragrant hops and thick, sweet malt;
in a welcoming horn of mead or ale, offered
to any who pass through the door; in a warm hearth-fire;
in tables weighed down with meat and bread, enough for all;
in guest-beds piled thick with quilts and soft pillows;
in tales told long into the night, in the laughter
of companions old and new, in comfort and in frith.
Hail the host of gods, the god of hosts! Hail Aegir!

Aegir

make welcome the guest

Hail to merry Aegir, best of brewers
whose ale and mead flows ever freely,
whose open hand and hearty good cheer
make welcome the guest and the traveler.
In your gold-lit hall the gods take their ease,
as the fine ale pours itself into each horn.
Aegir, the dark depths of the sea are yours,
and the wild waves frothing far above,
your nine fair daughters, each a treasure,
each a sailor's dream. Hail to Aegir!

Balder

fairest of the Aesir

Hail to bright Balder, son of farseeing Frigga
and wandering Odin, husband of faithful Nanna,
master of high-walled Breidablik. Shining Balder,
most praiseworthy god, fairest of the Aesir,
noble guest of kindly Hella, we honor you.
Balder, near-invulnerable one, of you
a tragic tale is told: your mother's gift
of protection, of a shield against all weapons,
proved no safeguard from tricks and treachery;
your death, in your own dreams foretold, came to pass,
inescapable despite all her efforts,
all her love and care. Balder, dweller in Helheim,
shining hope of the gods, both within and without
you hold a place. Hail to Balder! Hail the best of gods!

Balder

fair fame and good repute

Hail to Balder, Odin-son, best and brightest,
much-loved god whose fair fame and good repute
only reflect a kind heart, a true mettle,
an honor unblemished, a worth unsurpassed.
Master of Breidablik, most splended of halls;
son of fair Frigga, husband of Nanna.
In dreams you saw your end and the worlds';
brave Balder, honored guest in Helheim's depths,
patiently you wait for the far-away day
of your return, of the worlds' rebirth. Hail Balder!

Bragi

quick of temper and of tongue

Hail to Bragi, old one, kind one, finest of skalds!
Long-bearded As, quick of temper and of tongue.
wise one who knows when and how and of what to tell,
canny one who sees clearly and speaks with direction,
Husband of fair Idunna, provider of youth
to all Asgard; kind patron of poets and bards,
of those who sing and play in hall or hof. Bragi,
master of verse, rune-tongued weaver of many tales,
you grant to mortal men the gift of eloquence,
of rhetoric, of fiery prose, of ease and grace,
of freely-flowing words, of a firm grasp of meaning:
Bragi, we thank you, and ask your favor. Hail Bragi!

Bragi

rune-tongued master of stories

Hail to Bragi, wise one, long-bearded one,
word-weaver, tale-spinner, best of bards,
most skillful of skalds. Bragi, learned one,
rune-tongued master of stories and songs,
a merry tale can you tell in a trice,
or one to bring quick tears to all eyes.
With sweetened words you make welcome the guest,
with nimble wit you shift the minds of men.
Bragi, whose spark we seek, whose fire we crave,
whose touch we know but rarely. Hail Bragi!

Eir

cooler of fierce fevers

Hail to Eir, gentle goddess, best of all doctors,
cooler of fierce fevers, mender of shattered bones,
guide of the physician, the midwife, the surgeon--
the healing of all afflictions is in your power.
Wise in herb-craft, in the remedies of the earth,
your touch the cure for any ailment, your wisdom
the source of renewal and recovery
for any who seek it. Eir, kind-hearted goddess,
your gifts a sound body and a peaceful mind,
you ease our suffering, you take away our pain,
you give us the strength to beat back all ill health,
you restore us, you return us to a full life.

Forseti

upholder of justice

Hail to Forseti, master of Glitnir,
son of bright Balder and faithful Nanna,
wise one, fair one, upholder of justice,
arbiter, mediator, peacemaker,
to you do we turn when grievances
grow great, when tempers grow short
and battles seem unavoidable.
To you do we turn when a cool head,
a steady voice, a calm, reasoned,
balanced point of view are scarce. To you
do we turn for an evenhanded
decision. Forseti, clear-thinking god,
in you we trust for a sound resolution
to the most heated conflict. Hail Forseti!

Forseti

level head and even hand

Hail to Forseti, son of bright Balder
and kind-hearted Nanna, master of Glitnir,
wise one whose level head and even hand
bring peace to those driven by quarrels
and feuds, whose certain sense of the just
and the fair resolves all disputes.
Yours is the best of courts, Forseti,
god of the pure spring, god of the swift tongue,
sense-speaking god who brought the law to men,
strife-stiller, frith-bringer. Hail Forseti!

Frey

you gave your sword for love

Frey I hail, great god of harvests,
giver of wealth to men and land,
for fruit and grain we thank you now.
Husband of Gerd, you gave your sword
for love, a bargain you saw it.
I praise you now, O Ingvi-FreyR:
bring us bounty--give us peace.

Frey

peace without weakness

Hail to Frey, bestower of rich blessings,
lord of merry Yule, garlanded in green.
Joy is in you, and joy in us through you.
Frey, your gifts are many, your gifts are great:
for full bellies we thank you, harvest-god,
for children we have carried and borne,
for gold at need, for peace without weakness,
for lust and its fulfillment, for laughter,
for frith, for life's sweetest, purest moments--
for all these we thank you, kind Vanir lord.
With our happiness tonight, we thank you,
Frey; with our fellowship we honor you,
with our love for each other we know you.
In all good things we see you, gentle Frey;
for all good things we thank you. Hail Frey!

Frey

giver of field-wealth

Hail to Frey, giver of field-wealth, bringer of life
to the greening land, of peace and frith to mankind.
Frey, we know you in winter, your joy shining through
the bleak grey skies, warming the ice-laden trees;
in the hesitant spring we see you plainly,
as we dig in the chill earth, watching bare branches
sprout pale leaves, thinking of the rich harvest to come--
your gift, O Frey, for which we thank you with full hearts.

Frey

granter of lust and new life

Hail to Frey, kind-hearted, well-honored Van!
We welcome you, we ask your blessing.
Protector and provider of field
and farm, granter of lust and new life
to men and beasts, the cold earth herself
responds to your touch, bears fruit and grain.
Mighty Frey, stronger still in summer,
peace and pleasure and all that lives
and grows are your gifts. Hail to Frey!

Frey

a prize worth any price

Hail to Frey, fair Vanic lord, holder of Alfheim,
son of seafaring Njord, brother of bright Freyja.
Frey, much-loved god, provider of peace and plenty,
open-hearted one, drawn by instinct, by passion's fires,
who knows love's true value, a prize worth any price.
Mighty in battle, rich in the gifts of the earth,
lender of strength to the farmer's back, of profit
to his stead, of luck to his household. Ingvi-Frey,
giver of frith to mankind, of fruit to the land,
of the pleasure of bodies, of lust pure and clear,
of touch and taste and scent. Through your might we survive,
through your good will we grow and thrive. Hail Frey!

Frey

your touch on fruit and field

Hail to Frey, god of the green, god of growth
and new life! In summer we see you with ease,
your touch on fruit and field plain to all;
among winter's bare trees and ice-covered fields
your presence is less overwhelming, less clear,
but no less needed, no less trusted,
no less sure. Frey, bringer of joy, of pleasure,
of having enough, of riches of all sorts,
we thank you for your many gifts,
for the food on our table, for the love
of friends and family, for comfort and lust
shared with lovers, for passion and drive,
for feeling and sensation, for pure, raw life.
Hail to Frey! Hail to the giver of plenty!

Frey

the trickle of desire

Hail to Frey, shining son of noble Njord,
brother of incomparable Freyja,
rider of gold-bristled Gullinbursti,
pilot of swift-skimming Skidbladnir,
master of Alfheim, wielder of the antler!
Brave Frey, devoted husband of fair Gerd,
in a distant land you saw the white-armed maid
and were stricken--any price would you pay,
any sacrifice would you freely make,
to gain the heart of the giant's daughter.
Single-minded pursuer of true love,
we see you in the seasons' changing,
in all the rhythms of our bodies;
we feel you in the trickle of desire
along the spine, deep in the belly.
Driven by need, we know your might,
we know the keen-edged claim of passion,
a claim fierce and full, as dear as breath:
the call of lust is the call of life.
Forceful one, irresistible one,
your persuasion is of the earth--
we feel it in our frailty, our flesh,
our bones, our rushing blood. We know it
as we know we live. Frey, sower of seeds,
granter of gifts simple and sublime,
of the world and of the spirit, we honor you.
Hail to Frey! Hail the bringer of joy,
of renewal, of completion! Hail Frey!

Frey

green meads and wild woods

Hail Frey, lord of the fields we sow and reap,
lord of the beasts whose lives sustain our own,
lord of the light-elves, of the green meads
and wildwoods of Alfheim, yours as a tooth-gift.
We thank you for the gifts of the earth,
who cares for us as we care for her.
We thank you for the needs of the body,
the cravings that drive us ever toward life.
Hail to Frey, granter of good, fair-faced Van
whose hand we see in the growing world.

Frey

with fondness and with frith

Hail to fair Frey, god of the ever-green,
god of good fellowship, god of good cheer!
With blood-kin and heart-kin we join this night,
to hold a horn in hand, to drink deep,
to remember those beloved ones
from whom we are parted, to share the joy
of this holy season with those we hold dear.
With fondness and with frith we gather,
with feast and with folly we fill the long night.
Frey, to you we give thanks for our good fortune,
for the bounty we receive from the deep earth,
for the pleasure we take in good company,
for those who warm our beds, for those who know
our hearts, for the good strong drink that warms us
and the well-filled larder that keeps us strong
throughout the barren winter. Hail to Frey!

Frey

honey taken from the hive

Hail to great Frey, god of the good, god of the green,
gracious one from whose hands fall wealth of all kinds,
mighty Van, granter of gold, giver of grain,
a half-year past we saw your strength in fruited trees
and fields of grain, in honey taken from the hive.
Now we see you in the evergreen, in the tracks
of winter's beasts in fresh-fallen snow. Fair-haired Frey,
son of ring-giving Njord, husband of white-armed Gerd,
in a well-filled larder we know your might;,
in the joy of a cold night's company, a friendly horn
and a well-laden table, we know your kindness
and your gifts. Abundance is yours, O Frey!
For sufficiency we thank you; for the pleasures
of the world we praise your name. Hail to bright Frey!

Frey

holder of the seed

Hail to fair Frey, lord of verdant Alfheim;
son of noble Njord, most mighty of Vans;
suitor, then husband, of the peerless Gerd,
for whom your passion, headstrong and abiding,
drove from you all sense--your love for the maid
transcended reason, transcended duty,
as the call of life transcends the fear of death.
Holder of the seed, digger in the dirt,
god whose might draws each green shoot from the soil
and sparks desire in man and beast--Hail Frey!

Freyja

mother of all things

Sing I of Freyja,
chief of the Disir--
well-watchful women!
Chief of the Valkyr,
stern battle-maidens.
daughter of Nerthus,
mother of all things;
child too of Njord who
rules all the sea-depths;
sister of Frey, the
giver of field-wealth;
partner of Odin,
battle-slain sharer.
Wild, will-strong woman;
weaver of Wyrd and
wealth-wearing lady;
lover of love-songs;
lover of all love.
Strong women only
following Freyja!

Freyja

bearer of Brisingamen's might

Hail to Freyja, far-famed goddess,
giver of gold, lover of love-poems,
stirrer of strife, taker of war-dead.
Tears of gold you weep, fair Freyja,
bearer of Brisingamen's might.
I praise you now, great Vanadis:
grant us knowledge, grant us passion.

Freyja

sweet and bitter passions

All hail fair Freyja, peerless Vanir lady;
bright-eyed daughter of Njord, sea-god and wealth-bringer;
beloved sister of Frey, lord of field and folk.
Your beauty is far-famed, O radiant Vanadis:
many have longed for you, sought you as bride or lover,
but only to few have you given of yourself.
Glorious Freyja, shining lady of all love,
to you may we turn when our hearts are pierced or worn.
Yours are the arts of love, the pleasure of bodies,
the sweet and bitter passions that compel us all.
Golden-teared Freyja, bearer of Brisingamen;
Freyja, mistress of magic and stirrer of strife;
Freyja, incomparable goddess, I hail you!

Freyja

fire-eyed lady

Hail to Freyja, bright-haired goddess, fire-eyed lady
of power and passion. gold and amber tears you shed
for love lost; brilliant Brisingamen you bear
for might gained. Bold-hearted Freyja, beautiful one,
your loved desired by countless men, sought by many,
given for your own reasons, at your will alone.
Flawless goddess, your gifts abundant and vital
enrich and sustain our lives; we thank you for them.

Freyja
mistress of magics

Hail to Freyja, bright treasure of Asgard,
fair one, skilled one, sister of Ingvi-Frey,
beloved daughter of sea-loving Njord,
lover of Ottar, mate of wandering Od,
driver of cats, holder of Brisingamen,
strife-stirring woman, mistress of magics.
Radiant Freyja, many have sought you,
sought to claim your hand, your heart, your might.
Many have sought your wisdom, your lessons,
by your will alone may all these be given.
Freyja, glittering goddess, we thank you
for need that burns through us like white-hot flame,
for life-driven passion, precious as gold.
In warm skin and quickened breath we know you,
in a night of love and a lifetime's desire
we seize your gifts. Hail to Freyja!

Freyja
each tender moment a gift

Hail to Freyja, fair holder of Brisingamen,
mistress of cats, lover of Ottar, wife of Od,
child of noble Njord, sister of deep-hearted Frey.
Wielder of great magics, taker of battle-slain,
great Vanadis, your might is known throughout the worlds
and is felt throughout the lives of men and women.
We know you in love and need, in the heart's sharp edge,
in the depth of passion, in the clarity of pain,
each tender moment a gift, each agony
a lesson, each fall into passion a prayer
to Freyja, whose tears of gold fall for love long lost,
who knows her children like no other. Hail Freyja!

Freyja

sublime and destructive

Freyja, Vanadis, winner of Brisingamen,
mistress of Folkvang, hostess of battle-slain,
beloved of Ottar, bride of Od, free-hearted goddess,
friend of all lovers, granter of our darkest wishes,
for your blessings, countless, ceaseless, I thank you.
You inspire us to love, you kindle desire
in every heart, you persuade and provoke us
toward passions tender and savage, sublime
and destructive, transcendent and debased.
You set us into motion, pushing us toward
will and resolve, you move us to action,
you show us the vanity of indecision,
the folly of hesitation, the sorrow
of the missed chance. Freyja, glorious goddess,
you reach into our small sharp hidden places,
discovering our most secret fears, making them real,
exposing love's fragility, uncertainty,
necessity, its substance and its rarity.
You tear at wisps of ego, driving us to seek
within for what is firmly rooted. Golden-teared one,
destroyer of illusion, holder of hearts,
you goad us to take the next step, the first step,
you soothe us with love's treasures, you inflame us
with love's unreason, you hold us steady, Freyja,
as we walk between the paths of head and heart.

Freyja

games of love and of war

Hail to shining Freyja, driver of cats,
lover of Odin, bride of wandering Od,
holder of peerless Brisingamen,
holder of the hearts of lovers,
holder of the souls of warriors,
mistress of sturdy, high-walled Folkvangr,
goddess on whom we all call for aid
when love and lust have sent us to madness.
Glorious Freyja, fair one, free one,
mighty one, desirable one, peerless beauty
whose glance could shake the foundation
of any certainty, clear-sighted goddess
whose sharp eyes pierce any veil of feeling,
whose keen wit perceives what others may hide,
who knows the worth of pain in truth,
who knows the price of joy in falsehood,
who portions each as deserved, as proper.
Freyja, kind yet brutal, tender yet severe,
player at games of love and of war,
of all life's trials, you give to us the sharpest,
of all life's treasures, you give to us the sweetest.
Hail Freyja! Hail the Lady of the Vans!

Freyja

watchful wife of wandering Od

Hail to Freyja, warm breath of life,
child of earth and sea, amber-teared
goddess, strong-willed driver of cats,
watchful wife of wandering Od,
holder of Brisingamen's might,
chooser of the best of warriors.
With eyes soft or steely, your gaze
melts the strongest of us, bends us
to your will, persuasive Freyja.
With touch firm or gentle, your hand
guides those you favor to victory.
A tongue sharp yet sweet, a keen wit
ready for any challenge,
a depth of soul unmatched by any--
all these we know in you, fair one.
Bright-haired Freyja, we honor you.

Freyja

spark of lust in lovers' eyes

Hail to Freyja, noble mistress of Folkvang,
daughter of sea-faring, wealth-giving Njord,
sister of mighty Frey, granter of good,
holder of peerless Brisingamen,
driver of cats, skillful stirrer of strife,
desired by many, taken by none,
given only to few, only by your will.
Freyja, we know you in the spark of lust
in lovers' eyes, in each quick step toward self,
in the first heart-lightening signs of spring,
in all the needs that drive us together
and in all the needs that turn us away.
Gold-teared Freyja, beautiful goddess,
we thank you for your many gifts.

Freyja

your touch in wind and rain

Hail to shining Freyja, light of fair Asgard,
amber-teared goddess who holds the hearts of men.
Knowing one, canny one, you share with us
your might and your insight. Freyja, we feel
your hand guiding us through uncertain times;
we see your face in sea and sky, we know
your touch in wind and rain. Freyja, Vanadis,
battle-wise woman, hostess of war-dead,
wielder of magics both subtle and plain,
granter of boons to those you favor,
your courage and your wit inspire us.
Golden Freyja, fast friend of lovers,
yours is the first spark of any passion,
the ember kept warm through long winters, fanned
to flame anew each year in spring. Freyja,
we thank you for gifts granted, for hearts filled
and broken, for warm beds and warm bodies,
for the pleasures that bind us together,
that bring us to life. Hail to bright Freyja!

Freyja

wise and willful

Hail to Freyja, glory of fair Asgard!
We welcome you, we ask your blessing.
Bearer of peerless Brisingamen,
embodiment of unknowable might;
you know of those things that drive us most,
the desires that compel our survival.
Wise and willful Freyja, driver of cats,
mistress of far-famed Folkvang, granter of
our most heartfelt wishes. Hail to Freyja!

Freyja

tears of red gold flow freely

Hail to Freyja, glorious goddess, fair one, wise one,
    courageous and clever, mighty bearer
        of incomparable Brisingamen.
From the lands of the Vanir you came, Freyja,
    with knowledge dear and beauty unforeseen.
To the Aesir you brought these precious gifts,
Freyja, but all things of worth have their price,
    and all things in the worlds have their time
and their end. Freyja, whose tears of red gold
        flow freely, you measure loss by gain
            and gain by loss, each taken in turn,
            a sorrow but not a regret. Freyja,
    who bears the weight of sacrifice; Freyja,
    who knows the strength of desire; Freyja,
    mistress of might both devious and direct,
        I praise you for all you are, I thank you
    for gifts granted unasked, for fires that rage
within us, for thirsts unquenched. Hail Freyja

Freyja

soft voice hides an iron will

Hail Freyja, peerless goddess, honey-tongued one
whose persuasion and guile can charm all the world,
fair one whose soft voice hides an iron will
and a resolute heart. Freyja, whose hold
on the souls of men is firm, whose might
and wit are unrivaled in all of Asgard,
who knows the heat of desire and the chill
of love lost, we thank you for the sweetest
moments of life, for the passions that bring us
out of ourselves and into the divine.

Freyja

the cost of what we desire

Hail to Freyja, brightest bloom of Asgard,
great and mighty goddess, essence of passion.
Freyja, driver of cats, whose steady hand
guides us with subtlety and certainty;
Freyja, seeker of might and wisdom,
who teaches us to understand the cost
of what we desire; Freyja, granter of joy
and pleasure, who inspires us to relish
the gifts of the earth. Freyja, shining one,
who holds us in her arms, who sharpens our wits,
who for a precious moment lets us see
through her eyes the wonders of the worlds.
Freyja, daughter of the worthy Vans,
holder of mysteries, holder of wisdom,
holder of the brilliant Brisingamen,
we praise and honor you this day. Hail Freyja!

Freyja

wisdom, might and agile wit

Hail to bright Freyja, hail the Vanadis,
hail, goddess whose wisdom, might and agile wit
work wonders in the worlds. Hail Freyja,
whose steady hand makes sure the most headstrong
of beasts, whose radiance and grace make silent
the most eloquent of men. Hail Freyja,
whose voice we hear in the words of lovers,
whose heartbeat we feel in the throes of desire.
Freyja, shining Freyja, amber-teared goddess
who of love and pain knows all. Hail Freyja!

Frigga

friend of women

Hail to Frigga, Fensalir's mistress,
wise wife of Odin, all-knowing one,
Fjorgynn's daughter, household goddess,
spinner, weaver, friend of women,
who mothers call to ward our children.
I praise you now, O kindly Frigga:
bless our homes, our families.

Frigga

sorrowful mother

Hail to Frigga, wise and knowing wife of Odin,
sorrowful mother of bright Balder whose end
all your loving work and wisdom could not forestall.
Keeper and guardian of home and family,
we pray to you when we wed, when we birth our babies;
we call on you to bless our households, our children.
Maker of order, with a clean house and a warm meal,
with a full horn offered to each welcomed guest,
we honor you. Frigga, who knows and understands
all but keeps silent, who holds the keys of Asgard,
who is a constant friend of women, of mothers,
for refuge and support we call to you. Hail Frigga!

Frigga

holder of harmony

Hail to Frigga, hail the queen of Asgard!
Noble lady of bright Valhalla,
trusted companion of crafty Odin,
mistress of watery Fensalir,
guide of trusty, clever maidens--
Fulla and Gefjon, Saga and Eir,
Sjofn, Lofn, Vor and Var, Syn and Hlin,
Snotra and Gna, all brave and skillful maids.
Frigga, shrewd one who sees much, who knows much,
ever thinking, ever careful, acting
cautiously but swiftly, planning, dealing,
persuading, designing, doing all
possible to achieve your end. Frigga,
unsurpassed in wisdom, in insight,
in perception, in cunning and in judgment,
practical goddess who sees all options,
all opportunities, all divergent paths,
all fibers of Wyrd's sturdy fabric,
we call on you, goddess, for constancy,
for stability and certainty,
for order created and maintained,
as much as we may know in this world.
Hail Frigga! Hail the holder of harmony!

Frigga

holds knowledge dear as gold

Hail to fair Frigga, heart of every home!
We welcome you, we ask your blessing.
Keeper of the home, of the larder
that feeds us throughout the long, bare winter,
sharp-minded one, planner and provider,
through your gift of wit we outlast the cold.
Frigga, shrewd one who sees and knows all things,
who keeps her own counsel above all else,
who holds knowledge dear as gold. Hail to Frigga!

Frigga

holder of hard truths

Mighty Frigga, home of the heart, heart of the home,
lady of shining Fensalir, holder of hard truths,
you know the world and how it works, you know its folk,
you call us to do what we can, to do what we should.
Like a wise gardener, you know best the way to tend
each single seed. Like a good mother, you know best
the way to nurse each child, to kindle in their hearts
the fire of ambition, to teach them to dream
and to strive, to hold their hand, to nourish their soul.
Frigga, goddess of community, you grant to us
purpose, you grant to us hope, you guide us as we
find our way in the cold world. Goddess of common sense,
in reason and in judgment we see your hand; in wit
and in insight we know your wisdom; in foresight
and in feeling we hear your voice. Hail to Frigga!

Frigga

pulls order from chaos

Hail to Frigga, wise and knowing goddess,
great lady of Asgard, mistress of Fensalir,
whose guiding hand pulls order from chaos,
whose keen eye sees the patterns of existence,
whose presence makes our footing firm.
Beloved Frigga, fair one, judicious one,
wary and watchful, perceptive and aware,
guardian of children, defender of family,
holder of harmony, heart of the home,
we thank you for your blessings. Hail Frigga!

A Mother's Prayer to Frigga

bittersweet pain of parting

Hail to Frigga, careful one, sharp-eyed one,
friend of mothers, protector of children,
all-knowing goddess, all-watchful goddess.
You know the love of parent for child,
you know it is unshakeable, goddess,
you know it is everlasting. Frigga,
you know the joy of watching a child grow
into a fine man or woman, you know
the bittersweet pain of parting, you know
what is in a mother's soul. Frigga,
grant me a firm hand and a soft heart,
grant me understanding, grant me clarity,
grant me peace of mind in troubled times,
grant me the strength to bend with the storm
and emerge unbroken. Frigga, goddess,
grant my children the wisdom to choose wisely,
grant them the strength to stand firm against folly,
grant them the will to face any challenge,
grant them the wit to find their way in life.
Beloved Frigga, defender of families,
keep my children safe from harm, goddess,
ward them as they travel through the world.

To Frigga and Her Maidens

shield of the family

Hail to Frigga, mistress of the home and those within,
beloved lady of the hall, kind-hearted goddess
whose cool hand smooths the brow of the fevered child,
who comforts women in their travail, who grants
the gift of harmony and order to the house.
Friend of mothers who shares our joys and sorrows,
shield of the family, Frigga, I call to you.

Hail to mindful Saga, merry-hearted goddess,
wise and knowing mistress of deep-seated Sokkvabekk
teller of tales, drinker of strong ale and sweet mead,
granter of honeyed songs and well-spoken hails,
granter of eloquence, builder of discourse,
friend of the poet, the rhymer, the bard. Saga
of the pen, Saga of the word, I call to you.

Hail to Eir, best of physicians, best of nurses,
merciful goddess, healer of the wounded,
the feeble and the frail. Eir who sits upon
the healing hill, Eir who shelters the needy,
savior of the sick, maker of salves and healthful
remedies, with your soft voice and gentle touch
we soon grow whole and hale. Bright Eir, I call to you.

Hail to fair-haired Gefjon, goddess of the furrow,
wise one, knowing one, goddess who sees the ways
of Wyrd, for all the use that is to any being,
clever goddess who gladly fooled King Gylfi
and took the best of the old Dane's land. Mother
of strong sons you are, and yet a maid beside,
and care of maids is yours. Gefjon, I call to you.

Hail to Fulla of the flowing hair, dear sister
of noble Frigga who holds close the ashen chest
of Asgard's queen, who holds close her dearest secrets.
Singer of charms, granter of abundance, Fulla
who carries words of import and discretion,
Fulla who runs with swift and silent feet, who speaks
with Frigga's voice. Clever Fulla, I call to you.

Hail to kind-hearted Sjofn, who of love knows much,
who knows of hearts opened and souls merged, who knows
of the bond of affection on which family
is built, who knows of the devotion that holds
lovers together through good times and bad. Sjofn,
maker of matches, easer of the work of love,
granter of happiness. Sjofn, I call to you.

Hail to brave Lofn, whose spirit mild yet resolute
makes clear the road to love when trouble or obstruction
has barred the way, when fear or spite has denied it.
Gentle Lofn, untangler of knots, remover
of hindrances and snags, with steady step you lead
sweethearts and lovers into blessed marriage,
you stand against the foes of love. Lofn, I call to you.

Hail to Var the oath-keeper, whose name we give
to those weighty words we offer to the well,
whose blessings come to those who are true to their word,
whose vengeance falls on those who break that sacred bond.
Var, friend of the faithful, who hears all promises,
who stands behind all pledges, who guides us
toward honesty and honor. Var, I call to you.

Hail to wise and knowing Vor, careful goddess,
ever watchful, ever wary, ever seeking
the truth of all things. Cunning goddess, clear-eyed one
who sees what is, from whom no secret can be kept,
who understands the silences between our words,
Vor who knows much of intent and of action,
our hearts are open to your gaze. Vor, I call to you.

Hail to mighty Syn, guardian of the great gate
of Frigga's hall, heedful one who bars the door
against all ill, all wickedness, who forbids
the scoundrel and the wrongdoer from entry.
Keen-eyed Syn who knows the good man from the evil,
vigilant goddess who foils the wretch who would win
by means of treachery and lies. Syn, I call to you.

Hail to kind-hearted Hlin, friend of wise Frigga
whose work in the world you do, Hlin whose forewarnings
have saved many a man from defeat and despair.
The chosen of Frigg you ward from all harm, goddess;
you are the refuge of the weak, the champion
of the fearful, the protector of those who cannot
fight and those who cannot flee. Hlin, I call to you.

Hail to Snotra, wisest of the Asynjur,
wise in the ways of the worlds you are, wise too
in the ways of men; you know of custom
and of courtesy, you know the words that open
any door, you know the manner that pleases
kings and princes. Mistress of rhetoric, mistress
of protocol, honey-tongued Snotra, I call to you.

Hail to Gna, goddess of swift journeys, mistress
of nimble-footed Hofvarpnir who rides the winds
and the waves through all the worlds. Herald of Frigga,
you bear the gifts of Asgard's queen to all who find
her favor, her words you carry with all care,
fleet-flying through storm clouds, touching the tallest trees
you make your way. Bold and fearless Gna, I call to you.

To Frigga's Handmaidens

Hail to Saga, mistress of watery Sokkvabekk,
drinking companion of wandering Odin,
skillful teller of tales, holder of history,
deep source of wisdom gained by experience,
Quick-witted Saga, shrewd and sage, reasoned and profound,
the mead of inspiration is your drink. Hail Saga!

Hail to Eir, calm and gentle purger of all ills,
most skillful of doctors, most mighty of healers,
all cures and remedies are within your power.
Kind-hearted restorer of health to the stricken,
of hope and renewal, of strong bodies and sound minds,
for a good and active life we thank you. Hail Eir!

Hail to Gefjon, kind-hearted friend of maidens,
protector of innocents, guardian of the young;
in your hall dwell those who have passed from life unwed.
Clever taker of Zealand, beguiler of kings.
plough-woman, driver of oxen, mother of strong sons,
wide-ranging your interest, abundant your gifts. Hail Gefjon!

Hail to Fulla, sister and dearest friend of Frigga,
guardian of her treasures, sharer of her secrets,
holder of her trust. Fulla of the flowing hair,
the power of knowledge is yours; you understand
the obligations of necessity. Fulla,
fulfiller of wishes, provider of needs: Hail Fulla!

Hail to Sjofn, nurturer of love and desire,
of fast friendship and firm family bonds.
Frith-weaver, friend of lovers, the course of passion
is made clear by your hand--affection and devotion
are your gifts to mankind. Sjofn, you reveal to us
the urgent callings of the heart. Hail to Sjofn!

Hail to Lofn, gentle advocate of all love,
persuasive one whose art and wit may win
the right to wed for any who ask. Lofn,
smoother of rough roads, remover of obstacles,
shifter of burdens, diminisher of troubles,
you help us along dark paths, through tangled lives. Hail Lofn!

Hail to Var, who upholds the oaths of men and women,
who watches carefully those who pledge their word,
who ensures that that word is kept, who punishes
the oath-breaker. Promises and contracts, solemn vows,
honor, truth, fidelity, all are your concern,
firm-handed and trustworthy goddess. Hail to Var!

Hail to Vor, canny one from whom no secret can be kept,
wise woman, seeker after knowledge, finder of truth.
Clever one, quick to see and quick to understand,
open-eyed and clear-witted, cunning and discerning,
all things are revealed to you, no matter how long
and deeply buried, how skillfully veiled. Hail Vor!

Hail to Syn, who bars the door against all foes,
who welcomes friends but sends away those without,
whose spite or ill nature would endanger those within.
Shrewd and insightful warder of boundaries,
safe-keeper, defender of the falsely accused,
holder of the home, guardian of the family. Hail Syn!

Hail to Hlin, protector of those favored by Frigga,
vigilant guardian of those most dear to her heart,
you know her mind, you share her joys and agonies.
With care you watch over the sons and daughters
of mankind, you keep them safe from all danger,
you drive away all evil, you battle any foe.

Hail to Snotra, wise in the ways of the world,
quick of thought and clever of speech, smooth-tongued goddess
whose broad understanding and able diplomacy
may accomplish much. You know much of tradition,
and of when to hold and when to break with it,
your words as swift and sharp as any sword. Hail Snotra!

Hail to Gna, swiftest and trustiest of couriers,
tireless one, well-traveled goddess, you know the path
to every home, you find your way to every land
without fail, delivering each message with speed.
Rider of Hofvarpnir, flying over sea and sky,
you carry the words of Frigga to all the worlds.

Heimdall
final foe of Loki

Hail to Heimdall, watchful guardian of broad Bifrost,
son of the nine mothers, son of the cresting waves,
master of Himinbjorg, rider of swift Gulltopp,
wakeful holder of the world-piercing Gjallarhorn,
restorer to Freyja of peerless Brisingamen,
wary opponent and final foe of Loki.
Brilliant Heimdall, father of men, teacher of runes,
far-seeing and fore-seeing gatherer of facts,
clear-headed and diligent, trustworthy warder,
exacting friend of those who seek learning and lore,
stern and straight-backed defender of order,
you sustain the ideal, you drive the intellect.

Heimdall

shaper of mankind

Hail to bright Heimdall, keen-eyed watcher
over Bifrost, bearer of the Gjallarhorn,
keeper of the gate, holder of the bridge,
first defender of peerless Asgard.
Heimdall, who hears the leaves fall from the trees
and the blades of grass pierce the rich soil,
honored father of men, shaper of mankind,
giver of magic, teacher of rune-craft,
fair-faced As, child of the nine mothers,
elder god, ancient one. Hail to Heimdall!

Hella

so dark and so fair

Gracious Hella, so dark and so fair,
so grim and so beautiful, we call you.
Mistress of Helheim, daughter of Loki,
guardian of bright Balder, you hold your own.
Hella, provider of bed and board,
hearth and home, to those who have passed from life,
we thank you for kindness to those we love,
our family of long ago, our dearest kin,
our honored dead who dwell within your halls.
Hella, to whom we all may one day go,
friend of those who have died and those who weep,
we honor you now as the days grow short,
as night falls quickly and lasts so long,
as in this season the world itself falls cold.
Hella, we ask your presence tonight,
as we speak of our beloved dead.
As we remember them, we know your might.

Hella

granter of the last great gift

Remember death, remember kind Hella,
guardian of those who have passed from this world,
comforter of those who have left life and love
behind, reuniter of families,
generous holder of many-roomed Hel,
hostess to be of so many who now live.
Hella, seductive one, awesome one,
granter of the last great gift we may receive,
provider of all hospitality,
your hearth ever warm and welcoming,
your tables ever heavy with food,
your casks ever filled with mead and ale.
We thank you, Hella, for your kindnesses
to those we have loved during life and beyond,
for the certainty of your welcome,
for a warm safe place when our lives on Midgard
have run their full course. Hail to Hella!

Hella

as welcoming as one's own front door

Hail to Hella, alabaster goddess,
grave hostess to many who have walked
the long path to death, to reunion
with long-gone kith and kin, with folk unmet
until we pass from this existence.
The soothing touch of cool white hands, Hella;
the last sharp breath of one whose time has come;
the comfort of a loved one's spark of presence
in a long and cold and lonely night;
the longed-for meeting of beloved friends,
hands clasped and horns passed at your open hearth;
the reward of rest after hard-lived life;
all these are yours, sweet and solemn Hella.
Gracious Hella, as kind as necessity,
as welcoming as one's own front door,
as just and as true as nature itself,
we thank you for your many blessings.
your gift of release, your care of those
now gone from our lives. Hail to Hella!

Hella

preserver of Balder

Hail to Hella, hospitable goddess
rejoiner of families, of parted friends.
Mistress of Helheim, preserver of Balder,
provider of light and warmth to those
who wander in a cold, dark afterworld,
granter of rest and comfort to those
whose lives were long and hard and filled with strife.
We thank you, goddess, for your kindnesses
to those we have loved and lost, who have passed
from our world into yours. Hail to Hella!

Hella

guardian of the worlds' renewal

Hail to Hella, kind-hearted Hella,
who welcomes each traveler to her realm,
who carries sweet mead to those who thirst,
whose tables groan with good meat and bread,
with a place for each by a warm hearthfire,
as family and friends long lost gather round,
to hold the new one close, to clasp their hand,
for a heavy heart--a loss in one world--
brings joy and reunion in the next.
Hella, goddess, lady of Helheim,
heedful guardian of the worlds' renewal,
we thank you for your goodness and graciousness,
for your care of those who have gone before us
into the unknown. Hella, we hail you!

Hella

gate held firm against all ill

Gracious Hella, noble lady of the afterworld,
defender of bright Balder, kind-hearted guardian
of those who have entered your realm. Child of chaos,
keeper of order, mistress of the roomy halls
of shining Helheim, guardian of the frigid plains
of Niflhel, your gate held firm against all ill.
To our beloved dead you show your face so fair;
your fearsome visage you reserve for those whose evil
carries them to Nastrond's shore. Hella, best of hosts,
open-handed receiver of guests, your hearth
and your table you share with those who have passed
into your domain. Hail to Hella, hail the holder
of hope! We thank you for the blessings you grant to those
we have loved in this world, we thank you for a welcome
still to come. Hail to Hella, hail your safe haven!

Idunna

all will grow and be again

Hail Idunna, fair bride of long-bearded Bragi,
generous goddess, holder of the sweet fruit of youth.
Your might sustains the strength and vigor of the gods,
your beauty and spirit lend light and life to Asgard.
Cherished by the Aesir, coveted and sought
by envious giants, your presence a blessing,
your absence a grief, your theft a treachery.
Idunna, shining goddess, renewer of life:
in the seasons' change from cold to warm and back again;
in flowers that grow and fade, one after the other;
in trees that blossom, bear bright fruit, drop their brilliant leaves;
in faith that all will grow and be again, we know you.

Idunna

stolen by greedy Thiazi

Hail to Idunna, bright bloom of Asgard,
beloved wife of long-bearded Bragi,
watchful guardian of the sweet apples
of youth and vigor. Fair Idunna,
stolen by greedy Thiazi you were,
but by Loki's wit and Freyja's cloak
you were returned, holding close the treasured fruit.
Idunna, who knows when to speak in company
and when to keep silent, whose lightest touch
cheers the heart and lightens the step. Hail Idunna!

Jord

moss and roots and buried bones

Hail to Jord, mother of Thor who gave to her son
her strength and her solidity. Goddess of dirt
and sturdy stone, of moss and roots and buried bones,
of seed and stem, of cave and plain, of every patch
on which we step, on which we live our lives. Upon
your flesh we stand. We laugh and weep, couple and contend,
suffer the bitter and savor the sweet,
birth our babies, teach our children, bury our dead.
All our joys and sorrows, all that we love and fear,
all that we ever know, all comes from you.
Mighty Jord, encompassing goddess, we honor you.

Jord

holder of memories long fallen into the well

Hail Jord, soul of the deep earth, mother of red Thor,
fair as the white-tipped mountains, the soft green moss
that clings to rock and tree, the slow-flowing glacier
that carves the world like a sculptor's knife. Ancient Jord,
pulse of Midgard, in our bones and our blood we feel
your might, with every breath we take you in,
with every step we know your strength. Constant one,
steady one, cradle of humanity, granter
of gifts, taker of lives, destroyer of cities,
cleaver of stone, holder of relics of creatures
long gone, long forgotten, holder of memories
long fallen into the well. Jord, fair etin-maid,
strong of arm, strong of heart, strong of spirit to bear
the friend of men, I thank you for your patience
and restraint, I thank you for my life within yours.

Nanna

most steadfast and devoted of lovers

Hail to Nanna, strong-hearted bride of bright Balder,
most loving of wives, most faithful of consorts,
most steadfast and devoted of lovers. Nanna,
courageous one, daring one whose perilous journey
would strike terror into other hearts; Nanna,
compassionate one, gracious one whose presence
brings comfort to all, whose gentle, certain hand
builds order from chaos; Nanna, resolute one,
balanced one whose steady heart creates a home
in any place you go, no matter how foreign,
no matter how desolate, no matter how alone.
Nanna, strong one, quiet one, whose gift of belonging
can soothe and enliven, cheer and console. Nanna,
who lightens heavy hearts, who brings together
those who have parted, we honor you. Hail Nanna!

Nanna

intrepid and bold

Hail to fair Nanna, daughter of Nepr,
wife of bright Balder, devoted and true,
mother of silken-tongued Forseti.
Might-giving goddess, intrepid and bold,
fearless and faithful, you followed your love
on his most daunting journey, to share
his fate and his life, wherever they lead,
to burn with him on the crested sea,
to dwell with him in the halls of Hella,
to rise with him at the end of all things.

Nerthus

your might in the sprouting of seeds

Hail Nerthus, deep-minded goddess, older than old,
fair as any flower, as flowing fields of grain,
as evergreen forests carpeted with needles.
Nerthus, in groves were you honored in times long past;
your travels among your people, your priests, your wain,
are all we know of you, all the knowledge given us
by a changing world and a changing time. Nerthus,
we see you in the rich black soil we turn over
each spring; we know your might in the sprouting of seeds,
the mating of beasts, the feeding of life on life,
in the bearing of children, the nurture of youth,
in our own thoughtless grasping for survival.
Nerthus, mother, trusted one, unknowable one,
we thank you for bread and for breath. Hail Nerthus!

Nerthus

your secrets still unknown

Hail to Nerthus, deep-rooted goddess,
heart of the Vanir, soul of the earth,
center and source of our existence.
Straight and true your wagon fared, Nerthus,
drawn by kind-eyed cows, veiled in fine cloth,
served by doomed men, your secrets still unknown.
Nerthus, ancient one, knowing one, mother of gods,
within the blood and bone of old Ymir
you dwell, from icy peaks to fiery depths.
Field and furrow, seed and soil, all are yours.

Nerthus
sees beneath all cloaks and masks

Hail to Nerthus, ancient and wondrous,
hidden goddess who holds her secrets close,
peace-bringing goddess whose presence forbids
quarrels and conflicts, and all devices
of war. Deep-rooted Nerthus, Vanic mother,
of your shroud and wain we know little;
of your hand in the world we see much,
but our grasp of your might is feeble.
Hail to Nerthus, who knows of seed and soil,
who sees beneath all cloaks and masks. Hail Nerthus!

Njord

fair weather and safe harbor

Hail to Njord, elder Van, father of golden Freyja
and brave Frey, husband of mountain-loving Skadhi.
Shore-dwelling god, lord of high-walled Noatun,
the crash of waves on smooth-worn rock, the white sea-foam,
the ocean depths as black as any moonless night,
the shrill cries of greedy gulls--all are dear to you.
Fair weather and safe harbor your gifts to seamen,
gold to provide home and hearth your gifts to all men.
Wise one, kind one, giver of blessings small and great,
of wealth with which to live well from the earth's bounty,
of land on which to keep our families safe and whole,
of trust and faith that our needs will be met: Hail Njord!

Njord

where the sand meets the sea
Hail to Njord, fair-footed lord of Noatun,
god of the seacoasts, of well-traveled paths
and of routes uncharted, of journeys unknown,
of merchants and traders, farmers and fishers,
of the wealth of the world in land and in gold.
Njord, who sees what is through Vanic eyes,
who we find where the sand meets the sea,
who carries the might of soil and stone,
whose good humor and openhandedness
are unmatched in all the worlds. Hail to Njord!

Njord

a match unsuited

Hail to Njord, elder Van who came to Asgard
long ago, when blood lay warm on the field
of battle, when As and Van matched might and wit,
each finding in the foe an equal and a friend.
Njord, bringer of peace, giver of wealth,
ally of merchants, fair-footed sea-god,
distant love of shining Skadhi, a match
unsuited, a heart held ever close;
Njord, who we know as we walk on the shore,
standing at once in sand and sea. Hail Njord!

Odin

(at Yule) take the course of wisdom

Hail to Odin, wandering this cold white night,
leading the fearful hunt through wild weather,
stirring storms out of clear skies, driving us
within to safety and warmth. This night above all,
we gather with family, with friends, with those
who have become both over time and trust.
On this night we take the course of wisdom,
we hold to our hearths, we shun the wilderness.
Among our kin we find comfort and strength,
among our kin we stand against the storm.
This night above all, we feel your force,
Allfather, leading that which we most fear,
holding them fast or free, as is your will.
this night above all, Odin, we praise you,
we honor you and all your host. Hail Odin!

Odin

contriver of intricacies

Hail to Odin, sharp-eyed holder of knowledge dear,
wisdom won and wisdom taken. Keen and cunning,
subtle of shade, grey of manner, grey of nature,
far-ranging your interest, far-reaching your hand.
Allfather, seeker of priceless understanding,
knowing one, risking much, seeing always the goal.
Careful maker of deals, always skirting each edge,
master with whom warrior and poet rashly trade,
victory for soul, a bargain perhaps. Odin,
shrewd one, contriver of intricacies, worker
of fragile humanity, builder of world's end,
guided by vision, driven by need. Hail Odin!

Odin

(at Yule) guide of that fearful host

Hail to Odin, rune-master, wisdom-seeker,
grey-clad traveler, far-seeing schemer,
always searching, always pursuing,
always one step ahead of the foe.
Master of the hunt, leader of the dead
on their long night's journey; the darkness,
the bitter cold, they drive us inside,
away from your path. The screaming,
battering, bone-chilling winds reveal your course;
the storm's white wall, thick and clinging,
hides your trail. Odin, guide of that fearful
host, keep your charges far from our door,
keep us safe, form and spirit, through this black night.
Hail to Odin! Hail to the wanderer!

Odin

endless gathering of knowledge

Hail to Odin, wise and knowing Allfather,
lord of sturdy, broad-halled Valhalla;
lord of brave warriors and cunning mages;
winner of runes, seeker of wisdom;
master of incomparable Sleipnir;
husband of flawless Frigga, well-matched woman;
father of shining Balder, best of gods;
brother of the clever son of Laufey!
Traveler, making your way through the worlds,
always learning, always planning, always
with your eye on the ultimate goal,
seeker of new paths, finder of loopholes,
strategist, charmer, defender, magician,
endless are your manipulations,
subtle your methods, intricate your schemes,
your art and guile are without equal,
your focus on the needful well known to all.
Odin, with wit as sharp as any sword,
with judgment as deep as any chasm,
with strength to bear any misfortune,
we honor your commitment to survival,
your endless gathering of knowledge,
your unfaltering drive toward victory.
Hail to Odin! Hail the far-seeing one!

Odin

(at Yule) the madness we hold deep within our soul

Hail to Odin, lord of the dead, lord of the Hunt,
god of the long view, of the small spark of insight,
of the madness we hold deep within our soul,
that which inspires us, that which transcends us,
that which drives us to the edge of understanding.
On this longest night, with horse and hound, you ride,
as within these walls we hold together, kin and clan,
throughout the storm, throughout the dark, throughout the night.
As the sleet cuts into our faces, we know you.
As the sky grows dark and deadly white, we know you.
As the bitter cold numbs our hands and feet, we know you.
As the shrill wind shrieks in our ears, a voice so fierce
and so familiar, we know you and all your company,
those souls and spirits who join your winter's ride,
who roam the land as we the living hide our eyes.
Hail to Odin, hail to the hunters, hail the Hunt!

Odin

(at Yule) walker of the nine worlds

Hail to Odin, far-seeing one, mead-maddened one,
sharp-witted one who knows what is and what must be,
who hung nine days on the windswept tree, who gave up
an eye to the fathomless well, Odin who holds
the Hunt in check, or looses the hounds to chase down
the luckless traveler. Odin, whose gifts to men
are fleeting, but all the more precious for it;
Odin, who walks the slender line of inspiration;
Odin, who does what is needful despite the cost:
on Sleipnir you ride, leading the fearful host,
master of the hunt, lord of the valiant dead,
walker of the nine worlds, we hail your might this night!

Odin

the long view taken

Hail to Odin, Allfather, breath-giver,
seeker of wisdom, seizer of knowledge,
a gift for a gift, value for value,
pain for insight, all you know well.
The sons and daughters of ash and elm
call to you, wise one of many names.
We give you thanks for our own might,
we give you thanks for the gift of will,
for choices offered, for the long view taken.
Hail to Odin! Hail the wanderer!

Ostara

ice melts at your gaze

Hail Ostara, white-clad maiden.
Snow and ice melt at your gaze,
flowers bloom with each soft step.
We who late have longed for spring-time,
we welcome you at winter's end.
I praise you now, O bright Ostara:
Earth's cold cover send from here!

Ostara

slowly but certainly you come

Hail to white-armed Ostara, flower-maid,
within winter's grasp we see, so faintly,
pale green against white, purple crocuses
piercing the snow, through a thin crust of ice,
slowly but certainly you come to us.
Fair Ostara, distant one, longed-for one,
soft-stepping one, we welcome you once more.

Ostara

the might of new life

Hail to Ostara, swift one, fair one!
We welcome you, we ask your blessing.
We watch bare branches still lined with white,
we step with care on the slick-packed snow,
waiting for the first pale leaves to sprout,
for timid crocuses to pierce the ice.
Ostara, in you we see the might
of new life, of what will be with time
and through hard work. Hail bright Ostara!

Ran

hostess most generous

Hail to Ran, sea-dwelling wife of mighty Aegir,
mother of the nine daughters, of Heaven-Bright
and Bloody-Hair, of Frothing-Wave and Welling-Wave,
of the Cold One and the Pitching One, of Foam-Fleck
and Riser and Billow, all maidens fierce and fair.
Mistress of Hlesey, lady of that bright-lit hall,
hostess most generous, greetings you give to guests
well-traveled, a horn you bear to each who enters
your door. Dark-haired Ran, fearsome beauty, friend and foe
of seafaring folk, safe passage your gift to those
you favor, swift taker of those who sink below.
Hail to Ran, whose hand reaches through the dark sea-depths,
whose hoard of sea-sunk treasure, of shining gold and jewels,
would rival any king's, whose open-hearted welcome
to those within your walls is assured. Hail to Ran!

Ran

stirrer of seas, stealer of souls

Hail to Ran, fair bride of noble Aegir,
who holds the keys to the finest of halls,
who guides the drowned man to his final rest,
with a seat by the hearth and a horn of good ale,
to feast and tell tales far beneath the storm.
Ran, whose well-knotted net is ever ready,
whose nine daughters roam the oceans at will,
stirrer of seas, stealer of souls,
in the rush of waves we hear your voice,
in the sharp salt spray we feel your touch.

Sif

provider of fruitfulness

Hail to Sif, golden-haired bride of red Thor,
whose beauty and goodness are known to all,
whose touch brings life to our cold northern lands.
Fair Sif, whose tales are yet unknown to us;
gentle Sif, provider of fruitfulness;
Sif, who holds the heart of red-bearded Thor!
Sif we honor! Sif we praise! Hail to Sif!

Sif

protector of home and family

Hail to fair Sif, gentle bride of friend Thor,
mother of brave UllR and comely Trude.
Beautiful you are, your hair of fine gold
a treasure of unsurpassed value and need.
Guardian you are, Sif of the rowan-tree,
staunch protector of home and family.
kind-hearted you are, life-loving goddess,
peace and plenty your gifts to humankind.
Wise you are, with eyes of a seeress,
all things dark and hidden are clear to you.
Gracious lady, we thank you for your gifts,
the heavy-fruited trees, the fields of grain.
Sif, golden-haired granter of rich harvests,
shining goddess of hearth and kin--Hail Sif!

Sif

faith and hope within chaos

Hail to Sif, treasure of Asgard, beloved of Thor,
peerless prize sought in vain by greedy giant-kind,
whose hair of true gold falls to earth in bright waves.
Mother of brave UllR and beautiful Trude,
fair goddess whose might draws life from the soil,
warder of folk and kin, in you we know the heart
of family close by and long gone, in you we find
solace in despair, faith and hope within chaos,
a soft and gentle touch, a refuge from the storm.
Shining Sif, far-seeing one, wise one who knows much,
ancient one, kind one, protector of children,
frith-weaver, peace-bringer, holder of the home. Hail Sif!

Sif

kindness to desperate hearts

Hail to Sif! Shining one, gentle one, bride of Thor,
of dwarven gold your hair was forged, a treasure
of unparalleled worth, of might beyond telling.
Sif, kind-hearted goddess, provider of plenty,
of growth, of new green leaves on sun-warmed branches,
of sweet-scented roses, grapes thick on their vines,
of trees heavy with fruit, gardens rich with produce,
of the harvest's long days of labor, sweat repaid
with food enough to last throughout the winter.
Glorious Sif, home-loving one, defender of family,
of community, of bonds of love and friendship,
maintainer of precious frith, granter of great gifts,
we thank you for security, for steadfastness,
for safety and sufficiency. Bright-haired goddess,
clever one whose soft words and soothing voice
can still a storm of savagery, we thank you for
your many blessings, for your calming influence,
for your warmth and kindness to desperate hearts.
Sif, nourisher of body and soul, we honor you.

Sif

fields flowing with grain

Hail to Sif, warm-hearted bride of red Thor,
frith-weaving goddess whose hair of bright gold
lights any room, any land, any season.
Sif, none more fair walks the halls of the gods,
none more kind, none more necessary,
goddess whose might supports all existence,
your power coveted by many foes,
defended by all within the walls
of Asgard, honored by all who depend
on your strength and goodness for our lives.
Sif, bringer of bounty, provider
of rich harvests, of fields flowing with grain,
of trees heavy with fruit, of a winter's worth
of meat and bread, our survival resting
in your soft, sturdy hands. Shining goddess,
we thank you each day for your many gifts,
for our prosperity, for our lives.
Hail to Sif! Hail the giver of good!

Sif

hands hold the heart of the thunderer

Hail to Sif, shining light of fair Asgard,
whose soft voice speaks words of wisdom and might,
whose gentle touch guides subtly but firmly,
whose hair of true gold shines like the sun.
Incomparable Sif, bride of red Thor,
whose hands hold the heart of the thunderer,
mother of children both comely and strong,
compassionate goddess, who holds each child
within her arms, who shows us the substance
within our souls. Hail Sif, steadfast goddess!

Sif

unsurpassed in all the worlds

Hail to Sif of the yellow hair, whose will
it is that brings the fruited field to life
and to completion. Glorious bride of Thor,
fair flower of Asgard, treasure of the gods,
goddess unsurpassed in all the worlds,
in kindness and in goodness, in beauty
and in might. Sif of the rowan-tree,
Sif of the golden sheaf, Sif whose hand
we see in the earth's return. Hail to Sif!

Skadhi

bright jewels of ice on bare trees

Skadhi, winter's woman, we welcome you.
Soon cold winds will blow, soon snows will fall here.
Soon our land becomes yours, snowshoe-maiden.
Yours the beauty of pines hanging heavy,
yours the bright jewels of ice on bare trees,
yours the bright days when the sun hits white drifts,
yours the chill nights when together wolves sing.
Hail to Skadhi! Hail to winter's maid!

Skadhi

guide our arrows to their goal

Skadhi, clear-eyed huntress and bow-woman;
Thjazi's daughter, battle-maid avenging
with flashing sword his death; acceptor
of weregild; courageous and beautiful
bride of brave Njord, sea-god and shore-dweller
whose hall you left for the peaks of Thrymheim.
Dear to you are the howls of wolves, Skadhi,
dark lady who brings the snows of winter;
the fiercest storms and deadly ice are yours.
Guide our arrows to their goal, shining one,
keep us safe in our winter travels.
Hail Skadhi!

Skadhi

sharp eyes and steady hands

Skadhi, challenger of the gods, bright bride of Njord,
we welcome you. As green leaves turn brilliant in hue;
as each step grinds them, crisp and dead, into the earth;
as keen-edged winds tear at us, heralding your return.
Grant us safe travels through your season, O Skadhi,
keep our footing firm, our path straight on slick-smooth ice.
Grant us good hunting this year, shining bow-woman;
grant us sharp eyes and steady hands. Hail to Skadhi!

Skadhi

wild eyes flashing from the dark roadside

Hail to Skadhi, snow-shoe goddess, child of Thiazi,
seeker of vengeance, claimer of weregild, etin-bride,
in winter we know you in crisp-crusted snow,
in slick black ice, in knife-sharp winds, in bone-deep cold.
In summer we know you still in cold cloudless nights,
in close-grown woods, in shadowed clearings thick with moss,
in bright wild eyes flashing from the dark roadside.
Skadhi, wife of great Njord, companion of UllR,
brave huntsman with whom you share the wilderness,
kinswoman of shining Gerd, whose beauty compelled
the love of noble Frey. Skadhi, northern goddess,
wolf-friend, mountain-dweller, clear-minded one: Hail Skadhi!

Skadhi

woman of worth

Hail to Skadhi, fair bride of gods! Shining Skadhi,
strong is your sword-arm, deadly your blade. Thiazi's child,
vengeance-seeker, bold of spirit, clear of mind,
taker of weregild, woman of worth. Brave Skadhi,
keen-eyed huntress, your arrows swift, your aim unerring,
guide us in our hunting. Steady our hands, goddess,
quiet our footsteps, open our eyes. Winter's maid,
snowshoe goddess, surefooted on slick black ice,
ward us on our travels, keep us safe from storms.
In bitter cold, in knife-sharp winds, we feel your touch;
in bare trees sheathed in gleaming ice, in snows so white
they burn our eyes, we see your beauty. Hail Skadhi!

Skadhi

snows blow heavy and white

Hail to Skadhi, shining bride of gods,
seeker of vengeance, taker of weregild,
taker of what is rightfully yours.
Mountain-dwelling goddess, through thick snow
you make your way, quickly and cleanly
by snowshoe or ski, bow in hand,
ever watchful, ever wary.
Skadhi, of winter's ways you know much;
share with us your wit and vigilance,
your flawless aim, your endless vigor.
Watch over us when the winds are keen,
when the snows blow heavy and white,
when the roads grow slick and treacherous.
Brilliant Skadhi, guide our hands, our eyes,
our every step. Hail to fair Skadhi!

Skadhi

the fevered hunt to come

Hail to Skadhi, fair daughter of Thiazi,
strong-willed battle-maiden, bright bride of Njord,
mistress of Thrudheim, mountain-dwelling goddess,
warrior, huntress, unrivaled bow-woman.
Skadhi, in the northern lands we see you
always--even in the heat of summer
you never leave us, remaining always
in shadowy forests, in cold mountain streams,
in clear, cold nights, stars shining bright as jewels.
When the days grow bitter cold as well;
when the trees become brilliant with color,
their hues deceptively warm; when thoughts turn
to storing food, to gathering fuel,
to the fevered hunt to come--then, Skadhi,
do we know your strength in true, do we feel
your full force, do we enter your realm
of ashen frosts and shrill winds, of slick-iced paths
and waist-deep banks of snow, of long dark nights
by the fire, brutal storms raging and moaning
against the door. Skadhi, blood of giants,
child of discord, the choice to go within
the gates, to seize the world of order,
was given you. Weregild you took,
as fitting, as right; a husband you took,
joining with the clan of gods, with Asgard.
Goddess of our lands, goddess of our hearts,
we call to you! Hail to skillful Skadhi!

Skadhi

distant love of fair-footed Njord

Hail to fair Skadhi, bright etin-bride,
wolf-friend, mountain-woman, foe of chaos
who set the snake above the son of Laufey,
strong-willed and strong-hearted, self-sufficient
one who knows more than any the value
of community, the strength of family.
Skadhi, distant love of fair-footed Njord,
faithful daughter, your father looks down
upon you each night from the starry sky.
Skadhi, goddess of the snows, we hail you!

Skadhi

safe journeys through winter's gales

Hail to Skadhi, fair child of old Thiazi,
mountain-woman, bride of sea-dwelling Njord.
Skadhi of the snows, of a cold so keen
it sears the throat, of hard winds that drive
the stinging sleet against our faces,
of warm breath hanging in clouds before us.
Grant us firm footing on slick black ice.
Grant us safe journeys through winter's gales.
Grant us eyes to see your season's beauty.
Hail to Skadhi, ever-present goddess!

Skadhi

stand alone and prevail

Hail Skadhi, keen-witted daughter of Thiazi!
Steel-eyed goddess, fair-browed etin-bride,
bow-woman who strikes swiftly, surely,
with power and precision. Mountain-woman,
friend of wolves, whose distant howls bring comfort
and solace, who joined with the Aesir
not from need but from desire, for always
could bright Skadhi stand alone and prevail.
Peerless woman, strong of bow-arm, swift of shaft,
of worth and honor you know much. Hail Skadhi!

Skadhi

sharpened shafts and feathered flights

Bright-eyed Skadhi, daughter of the mountain-giant,
child of the snow and ice, wood-roaming goddess,
firm of footing, firm of purpose, firm of will.
We welcome you, we welcome your strength, we welcome
your season. Skadhi of the cold, shrill winds, the darkened
skies, the frozen earth, Skadhi of sharpened shafts
and feathered flights, stout-armed bow-woman, sure
of hand and sturdy of heart. Grant to us a keen eye
and a steady hand, grant to us full freezers
and safe journeys. Hail to Skadhi! Hail winter's maid!

Yule Eve Prayer to Sunna

together in safety

Farewell to bright-haired Sunna, friends, farewell!
With the long night's coming we turn away,
we turn toward home and hearth, toward friends, toward kin.
Together we stay 'til this dark night ends,
together in strength, together in safety,
'til morning comes and with it your return.
For light and warmth we thank you. Hail Sunna!

Yule Morning Prayer to Sunna

strength and certainty

Bright Sunna we see once more, be welcome!
the long night is over, again we look
to the sky without fear, without dread.
Together we held throughout the dark night
and together now we face the new day.
Your return releases us from our fear,
brings us strength and certainty. Hail Sunna!

Sunna

your favors fall freely upon us

Hail to Sunna, bright-clad rider in summer skies,
drawn through thickening clouds by faithful Shining-Mane,
your favors fall freely upon us until day's end.
Golden light-bringing goddess, your least glance warms us,
melts the last firm-packed snow within the darkest wood,
drives off the frost, turning crisp white grass green once more.
Brilliant Sunna, fair sister of grey-cloaked Mani,
at Midsummer dawn of old were great bonfires lit
to honor you and bring your blessings to the land.
On this longest day we gather here, O Sunna,
giver of life and of might. On this strongest day
we ask your blessing. Hail Sun-maiden--Hail Sunna!

Thor

rains you bring us

Thor I hail now, Mjollnir's master,
strong-armed husband of golden Sif,
son of Earth, son too of Odin.
Good friend Thor, helper of mankind,
rains you bring us, and then ripe fields.
I praise you now, great god of thunder:
bless our efforts, ward us from harm.

Thor

joys in feasting and fellowship
Hail to Thor, strong-armed wielder of Mjollnir,
whose might is well-known to friend and to foe,
who guards the lands of gods and men alike.
Great Thor, mightiest of all the Aesir;
friend Thor, who we turn to in time of need;
Thor, who joys in feasting and fellowship!
Thor we honor! Thor we praise! Hail to Thor!

Thor

we welcome the dark skies

Hail to red Thor, strong-armed defender of Midgard,
great-hearted friend of men, guardian of travelers,
bold wielder of Mjollnir, sender of wild spring storms.
Thor, son of the deep earth, son of far-seeing Odin,
ever-watchful guardian, foe of earth-rending chaos,
we welcome the dark skies, the blackness streaked with light,
the hard rains, the soft green life that follows.
Thor, red-beard, in you our faith is well-founded,
your gifts of strength and protection we hold most dear,
your clear sight, your good sense,
your sure aim, your straight talk,
all these we know, all these we prize, all these we seek
in our own lives. Constant and candid, true and trusty
Hail earth's safe-keeper!
Hail the rain-bringer!
Hail Thor!

Thor

nourish our lands

Hail Thor, constant defender of man!
We welcome you, we ask your blessing.
Strong-armed one, red-bearded storm-bringer,
we wait for winter's snow and sleet
to end, for your life-giving rains to come,
for the earth to return your gift
with her own. Thor, husband of fair Sif,
you keep us safe, you nourish our lands,
in you our faith is firm. Hail to Thor!

Thor

traveler through lands fair and foul

Hail to Thor, red-bearded warder, wielder of sky-fire,
oak-splitter, thunderer, stout holder of Mjollnir.
Friend Thor, trusted protector of men and women,
of those who journey far from home among strangers,
guardian of Asgard and Midgard both, we call to you
to keep us safe, to watch over our children,
to support our own best efforts and lend your strength
where our own may fail. Thor, keeper of the border,
of the line between those within and those without;
ever wise in the world's ways, tireless traveler
through lands fair and foul, of friend and foe alike;
seeker of the direct path, the sure road. Hail Thor!

Thor

matchless champion of frail humanity

Hail to Thor, defender of the great gods,
defender of men, warder of borders,
warder of the home. Master of lightning,
guide of storms, we call on you to keep us safe.
Friend Thor, husband of golden-haired Sif,
father of children strong and fair, Modi
and Magni and beautiful Trude,
travel companion of crafty Loki,
master of Thrudheim, opposer of etins,
wielder of irresistible Mjollnir,
with gauntlets of iron you prepare yourself,
with belt of might you gird yourself for battle.
Many tales tell of your feats of strength,
your courage, your wit, your aid to those in need.
Many tales tell of your constant struggle
to keep safe the walls of shining Asgard.
Red-bearded Thor, stalwart one, enduring one,
matchless champion of frail humanity,
we thank you for your protection. Hail Thor!

Thor

warding the worlds

Hail to red Thor, champion of Asgard,
wielder of Mjolnir, slayer of giants,
defender against the foes of order.
For bringing the rains, for warding the worlds,
for preserving the bounds, we thank you.
Thor, friend of man, defender of travelers,
son of crafty Odin and life-giving Jord,
husband of Sif of the golden hair,
father of those who will endure the end,
we honor you and all your deeds. Hail Thor!

Thor

master of the warm spring rains

Hail to Thor, red-bearded son of Odin!
We welcome you, we ask your blessing.
Slayer of giants, the foes of Asgard,
friend of the men and women of Midgard,
upholder of the order of the world,
wielder of the thunderbolt, bearer
of matchless Mjollnir, master of the warm
spring rains that bring the deep-sunk seeds to life,
master of the lightning. Hail to Thor!

Tyr

guardian of the word

Hail to Tyr, bravest of gods, guardian of the word,
keeper of honor, builder of the best of men,
upholder of the common good, of home and kin,
you give all that is needed, your thought not of self
but of all who rely on your wise decisions.
Tyr, maintainer of what is right, of what is best,
of what keeps those within safe and free from fear,
severe one, looking always toward the truly just,
only with hearts clean and clear may we call on you,
for those who seek your justice will gain your judgment.
Tyr, ancient one, worthy one, held throughout the worlds
in highest regard, mindful one, careful one: Hail Tyr!

Tyr

to serve both honor and need

Hail to one-armed Tyr, just one, noble one.
Hail Tyr, whose oldest tales remain untold;
hail Tyr, whose deepest roots remain undug.
A friend to the wolf you once were, O Tyr;
when called to serve both honor and need,
you chose the path of pain and loss, your hand
was taken--your word you kept. Tyr, who we
call on for justice, whose gifts are given
with an even hand, who knows which man
bears guilt and which is honest. Hail to Tyr!

UllR

shield-sailing sorcerer
Hail to UllR, glory of the Aesir.
So fair you are to look upon, UllR,
so peerless a bowman, so swift your skis.
Shield-sailing sorcerer, tamer of horses,
a warrior's gift may you bestow on those
you favor most, courage and strength and skill.
Yours is the yew-tree, yours the northern lands;
honored you are by your folk in the north,
welcomed with winter by hunter and tracker.
UllR, we call you to aid in our hunting.
Your people of snow and ice hail you now.
Hail UllR!

UllR

on broad fields and in tangled woods

UllR, glory of the gods, swift and surefooted
son of Sif of the golden hair, we welcome you.
On broad fields and in tangled woods we see your might,
snowshoe-god, hunter, bowman whose aim never fails.
Grant us good fortune, UllR, god of the far north,
as we tread on crusted snow, gun or bow at hand,
watching for quarry with which to fill our larder
and feed our families well. Hail to UllR!

UllR

your favor in this bitter season

Hail to UllR, son of Sif, glory of the gods!
Best of hunters, best of trackers, best of bow-men,
we ask your favor in this bitter season,
we ask your guidance as we seek our quarry,
we ask your wisdom as we make our way.
Grant us cunning, grant us vigor, grant us strength.
May our judgment be fine, our will firm, our wit quick.
We see you in the brilliant, shifting northern sky,
in shadows cast by thin-limbed trees, in days more dark
than light. We know you in fingers numbed, in hunger eased,
in hair made crisp with ice. UllR, god of the north,
god of the long winter, we welcome you. Hail UllR!

UllR

bow in hand, waiting for deer

Hail to UllR, master of Ydalir,
quick-thinking son of golden-haired Sif,
god of the winter, god of the north.
With skis strapped tight, with bow at the ready,
you travel, swiftly and certainly,
through thick-grown woods, branches bare
of leaves, coated with glittering ice.
In clouds of breath hanging still in the air;
in cold so piercing it stings our lungs
and numbs gloved fingers; in children's
sleds on well-packed hills; in grey mornings
spent crouched, bow in hand, waiting for deer,
UllR, we know you, we feel your might.
Hail to UllR! Hail the bow-god!

UllR

provider of meat to feed one's kin

Hail to UllR, son of golden-haired Sif,
fair-faced bow-god whose aim is ever true,
skilled hunter of beasts, provider of meat
to feed one's kin throughout the frozen months.
Snowshoe-god, agile one whose swift step
across sheer drifts is unmatched by any.
Share with us your keen eye and steady arm,
grant us a sure shot and a safe return,
as we join you in the winter's hunts.
Hail to UllR! Hail to the huntsman!

UllR

knows the ways of every beast

Hail to UllR, hail the god of the hunt!
Hail UllR, whose aim is ever true,
whose arm is strong, whose eye is keen,
whose step is sure in deep-drifted snow
or on treacherous ice, who roams the woods,
who knows each tree, each nest, each hiding place,
who knows the ways of every beast. UllR,
son of bright-haired Sif, bowman unsurpassed,
unyielding one who travels, free and fleet,
through winter's rage. Hail UllR! Hail the bow-god!

UllR

master of bright-halled Ydalir

UllR of the northern lands, UllR of the cold
and the stinging wind, bow-god, hunting-god,
deer-stalker, sharp-eyed tracker of bird and beast.
We welcome you, we welcome your strength, we welcome
your season. UllR, glory of the gods, bearer
of the oathring, master of bright-halled Ydalir
that stands among the green-boughed yew, rune-master,
son of Sif, elf-friend, wise and prudent chief. Grant us skill
and silence as we step on crusted snow, grant to us
a season safe from harm. Hail to lordly UllR!

Vanir Prayer

in frith with former foes

All hail the mighty Vans! From Vanaheim you came,
wise ones, knowing ones, rooted in the deep earth,
in sea and stone, in gold and grain, in life and lust.
In Asgard you dwell, fair-hearted gods of noble tribe,
to live in frith with former foes, to join your might.
Well matched in war, well met in peace, well known by all
within the worlds. Best of guests, finest of allies,
friends of the land-wights, who know much of what will be,
who know what lies within heart and soil. Hail the Vanir!

To the Vanir
a lusty nature and a merry heart

Hail to the Vans! Knowing ones, ancient ones, mighty ones
who in elder times broke down the walls of Asgard,
who trampled and tore the very field of battle,
who found in the noble Aesir an even match,
a wise accord, a balanced realm of friend and peer.
From Vanaheim your line arose--fair Vanaheim,
land of green mead and quiet wood, of waters deep
and barrows long enclosed. To bright-halled Asgard
came you four--Nerthus and Njord, Freyja and Frey--
to join your might with the fair Aesir, to share
with them your knowledge and your wisdom, to bring
to that land a lusty nature and a merry heart.
Farsighted gods of the Vanir, we thank you for
the roots that dig into the earth, for the black soil
beneath our feet and the seed that lies so deep within,
for the food we eat, for the daughters and sons
who bring joy to our lives and strength to our kin,
for each and every beat of our heart--for all this,
dear Vanir, we thank you. Hail the gods who bring life
to our lives! Hail the gods of shining Vanaheim!

To the Ancestors

lessons to treasure

Hail to those who have gone before, our honored dead,
our grandmothers and grandfathers of ages past.
Hail to those who have given their genes, those gifts
from men and women long gone that live on in us,
and to those who have given their love and their care;
whose stories have traveled through generations;
whose deeds and choices have founded our own lives.

Hail to those who have given their work and wisdom
to the world, whose efforts have built nations and
changed the path of history, whose actions have turned
the lives of others in small but essential ways,
those leaders and warriors, thinkers and believers,
farmers and teachers, builders and inventors,
artists and healers and tellers of tales.

Hail to those who have passed from this world to the next,
to those who dwell now within the halls of Hella,
to those who inspire us, to those we recall
with love, to those who watch over us with kind eyes,
whose lives have touched us, whose tales have moved us,
whose wisdom has granted us lessons to treasure.
Hail to the ancestors! Hail to the honored dead!

To the Ancestors

lost friends and long-gone kin

To all of those who have gone before us,
to all of those whose love we have known
and who we have loved, to all lost friends
and long-gone kin, to all of those whose blood
runs through our veins, whose faces we see
in our children, whose lives provide for us
inspiration and insight, without whom
we would not be, to our ancestors
of heart and of mind, of bone and of breath,
we remember you this night, we honor your lives,
we honor your wisdom, we find you in ourselves.
Hail the beloved dead--we remember you!

To the Ancestors

your spirit in our children's eyes

Beloved ones, friends and kin long gone, family lost
to time and distance, grandmothers and grandfathers
of centuries past, you whose loss still cuts knife-sharp
and you we know only from oft-repeated tales.
Honored ones, you whose lives inspire us, you whose deeds
shaped history for good or ill, whose blood
runs through our veins,
you whose bold and restless hearts brought us to new lands,
you to whom we owe our lives and our existence,
we remember you this night. We see your faces
in the mirror each day, we see your spirit
in our children's eyes. We see the world we live in
and recognize your hand in it; we find our way
through life and know your lives as well. Through the years
we hear your voice, we feel your gaze, we know your love
and care. Hail to the dead, hail to our foundation.

Rituals

Yule Rite to Frey

A Winterhof Yule is an all-night affair. We begin at sunset with a brief, informal horn to Sunna; in the evening we have a ritual to Frey, and at around midnight we honor Odin. The Frey blot is one of joy in the season, a reminder of all we owe to the beautiful Van, all the blessings he grants to us in summer that last us all through the winter.

NEEDED
Mead or other beverage
Drinking horn or other vessel
Blot bowl
Straw goat or pig, or evergreen wreath
Slips of paper for writing hopes and wishes
Pen
Yarn to tie papers to "messenger"

HALLOWING

May the hammer of Thor hallow and hold this place, and may Redbeard ward and watch over those gathered here today.

INTRODUCTION

Good Yule to all! On this longest night, we mark the end of the darkening year. Tomorrow the day will be a little bit longer, and the next day longer still, until the time when the green returns. And as the days grow longer, our sense of great Frey grows stronger. In the dark of winter we may not see him so clearly, but fair Frey is always here, the might and joy of the Vans is always with us.

OFFERING

Pour mead into horn.

Hail to great Frey, god of the good, god of the green,
gracious one from whose hands fall wealth of all kinds,
mighty Van, granter of gold, giver of grain,
a half-year past we saw your strength in fruited trees
and fields of grain, in honey taken from the hive.
Now we see you in the evergreen, in the tracks
of winter's beasts in fresh-fallen snow. Fair-haired Frey,
son of ring-giving Njord, husband of white-armed Gerd,
in a well-filled larder we know your might;,
in the joy of a cold night's company, a friendly horn
and a well-laden table, we know your kindness
and your gifts. Abundance is yours, O Frey!
For sufficiency we thank you; for the pleasures
of the world we praise your name. Hail to bright Frey!

Pass horn, pour out remaining mead into bowl.

BEAST/WREATH DEDICATION

*Here we present the straw beast (or evergreen wreath) to those
assembled; it will remain on the altar where anyone who wishes to can
write a wish or hope for the year to come on a slip of paper and attach
it to this "messenger," which will be burned at the end of the Yule
season.*

CLOSE

To bold-hearted Frey we offer our thanks and our joy. You have blessed us,
and in all ways we are richer for it.

The blot is ended; may we go forth and live well, firm in our faith and strong
in our bonds with our gods.

Yule Rite to Odin

This late night rite to Odin focuses on the old man's role as leader of the Wild Hunt. Most years the weather cooperates, and we can hear the wind screaming at the door as we pass the horn. As the Frey blot is a reminder of the joys of winter, the Odin blot recalls the many perils that are part and parcel of this season.

Mead or other beverage
Drinking horn or other vessel
Blot bowl

HALLOWING

May the hammer of Thor hallow and hold this place, and may Redbeard ward and watch over those gathered here today.

INTRODUCTION

In the cold, in the dark, on this long winter's night,
the Wild Hunt rides. The wind shrieks as with one voice
the riders call to us. We gather together
with friends and with kin, we gather together
against the storm, against the furious host.
Within these solid walls we tell our tales, we feast
and make merry, and take joy in each other,
and pay honor to the one who leads the dread band.

OFFERING

Pour mead into horn.

Hail to Odin, far-seeing one, mead-maddened one,
sharp-witted one who knows what is and what must be,
who hung nine days on the windswept tree, who gave up
an eye to the fathomless well, Odin who holds
the Hunt in check, or looses the hounds to chase down
the luckless traveler. Odin, whose gifts to men
are fleeting, but all the more precious for it;
Odin, who walks the slender line of inspiration;
Odin, who does what is needful despite the cost:
on Sleipnir you ride, leading the fearful host,
master of the hunt, lord of the valiant dead,
walker of the nine worlds, we hail your might this night!

Pass horn, pour out remaining mead into bowl.

CLOSE

Hail to Odin! Hail the huntsmen! We honor your calling, we honor your
might.

The blot is ended; may we go forth and live well, firm in our faith and strong
in our bonds with our gods.

Midwinter Rite to Frigga and Her Handmaids

There are a number of rites that modern Heathens associate with February. Some people do a blot to Thor to keep away the winter storms; others do a Disablot to the ancestors, and still others honor Vali's Day. In Winterhof we hold a rite to Frigga and her handmaids, because in the middle of winter we spend so much of our time in their world.

NEEDED
Mead or other beverage
Drinking horn or other vessel
Blot bowl
Crafting implements (knitting needles, spindles, etc.) to be blessed

HALLOWING

May the hammer of Thor hallow and hold this place, and may Redbeard ward and watch over those gathered here today.

INTRODUCTION

Winter's winds blow strong this time of year; even the snow that drifts against the door can't silence the sound. In these cold, dark days, we find ourselves living in the realm of Frigga. We find ourselves doing the work of Frigga. And in this time we find ourselves growing closer to Frigga, and to the wondrous goddesses who make up her retinue: tale-telling Saga, Eir of the healing hands, wise and knowing Gefjon, trustworthy Fulla, sweet-natured Sjofn and fierce-hearted Lofn, Var who holds us to our oaths and Vor who sees all that is true, Syn the guardian and Hlin the safekeeper, careful Snotra and fleet-flying Gna.

OFFERING

Pour mead into horn.

Hail to Frigga, mistress of the home and those within,
beloved lady of the hall, kind-hearted goddess
whose cool hand smooths the brow of the fevered child,
who comforts women in their travail, who grants
the gift of harmony and order to the house.
Friend of mothers who shares our joys and sorrows,
shield of the family, Frigga, I call to you.

Pass horn, pour out remaining mead into bowl.
Pour mead into horn.

Hail to mindful Saga, merry-hearted goddess,
wise and knowing mistress of deep-seated Sokkvabekk
teller of tales, drinker of strong ale and sweet mead,
granter of honeyed songs and well-spoken hails,
granter of eloquence, builder of discourse,
friend of the poet, the rhymer, the bard. Saga
of the pen, Saga of the word, I call to you.

Pass horn, pour out remaining mead into bowl.
Pour mead into horn.

Hail to Eir, best of physicians, best of nurses,
merciful goddess, healer of the wounded,
the feeble and the frail. Eir who sits upon
the healing hill, Eir who shelters the needy,
savior of the sick, maker of salves and healthful
remedies, with your soft voice and gentle touch
we soon grow whole and hale. Bright Eir, I call to you.

Pass horn, pour out remaining mead into bowl.
Pour mead into horn.

Hail to fair-haired Gefjon, goddess of the furrow,
wise one, knowing one, goddess who sees the ways
of Wyrd, for all the use that is to any being,
clever goddess who gladly fooled King Gylfi
and took the best of the old Dane's land. Mother
of strong sons you are, and yet a maid beside,
and care of maids is yours. Gefjon, I call to you.

Pass horn, pour out remaining mead into bowl.
Pour mead into horn.

Hail to Fulla of the flowing hair, dear sister
of noble Frigga who holds close the ashen chest
of Asgard's queen, who holds close her dearest secrets.
Singer of charms, granter of abundance, Fulla
who carries words of import and discretion,
Fulla who runs with swift and silent feet, who speaks
with Frigga's voice. Clever Fulla, I call to you.

Pass horn, pour out remaining mead into bowl.
Pour mead into horn.

Hail to kind-hearted Sjofn, who of love knows much,
who knows of hearts opened and souls merged, who knows
of the bond of affection on which family
is built, who knows of the devotion that holds
lovers together through good times and bad. Sjofn,
maker of matches, easer of the work of love,
granter of happiness. Sjofn, I call to you.

Pass horn, pour out remaining mead into bowl.
Pour mead into horn.

Hail to brave Lofn, whose spirit mild yet resolute
makes clear the road to love when trouble or obstruction
has barred the way, when fear or spite has denied it.
Gentle Lofn, untangler of knots, remover
of hindrances and snags, with steady step you lead
sweethearts and lovers into blessed marriage,
you stand against the foes of love. Lofn, I call to you.

Pass horn, pour out remaining mead into bowl
Pour mead into horn.

Hail to Var the oath-keeper, whose name we give
to those weighty words we offer to the well,
whose blessings come to those who are true to their word,
whose vengeance falls on those who break that sacred bond.
Var, friend of the faithful, who hears all promises,
who stands behind all pledges, who guides us
toward honesty and honor. Var, I call to you.

***Pass horn, pour out remaining mead into bowl.
Pour mead into horn.***

Hail to wise and knowing Vor, careful goddess,
ever watchful, ever wary, ever seeking
the truth of all things. Cunning goddess, clear-eyed one
who sees what is, from whom no secret can be kept,
who understands the silences between our words,
Vor who knows much of intent and of action,
our hearts are open to your gaze. Vor, I call to you.

***Pass horn, pour out remaining mead into bowl.
Pour mead into horn.***

Hail to mighty Syn, guardian of the great gate
of Frigga's hall, heedful one who bars the door
against all ill, all wickedness, who forbids
the scoundrel and the wrongdoer from entry.
Keen-eyed Syn who knows the good man from the evil,
vigilant goddess who foils the wretch who would win
by means of treachery and lies. Syn, I call to you.

***Pass horn, pour out remaining mead into bowl.
Pour mead into horn.***

Hail to kind-hearted Hlin, friend of wise Frigga
whose work in the world you do, Hlin whose forewarnings
have saved many a man from defeat and despair.
The chosen of Frigg you ward from all harm, goddess;
you are the refuge of the weak, the champion
of the fearful, the protector of those who cannot
fight and those who cannot flee. Hlin, I call to you.

Pass horn, pour out remaining mead into bowl.
Pour mead into horn.

Hail to Snotra, wisest of the Asynjur,
wise in the ways of the worlds you are, wise too
in the ways of men; you know of custom
and of courtesy, you know the words that open
any door, you know the manner that pleases
kings and princes. Mistress of rhetoric, mistress
of protocol, honey-tongued Snotra, I call to you.

Pass horn, pour out remaining mead into bowl.
Pour mead into horn.

Hail to Gna, goddess of swift journeys, mistress
of nimble-footed Hofvarpnir who rides the winds
and the waves through all the worlds. Herald of Frigga,
you bear the gifts of Asgard's queen to all who find
her favor, her words you carry with all care,
fleet-flying through storm clouds, touching the tallest trees
you make your way. Bold and fearless Gna, I call to you.

Pass horn, pour out remaining mead into bowl.

BLESSING OF CRAFTING TOOLS

Anyone who has brought a crafting implement may place it on the altar.

Mighty Frigga and all the Asynjur,
great goddesses who rule the domain
of women, we ask your favor. In winter
we live our lives close to home, and in this
quiet time, as we bar the door against
the storm, we busy our hands with fleece
and yarn and other works of craft and art.
Grant to us, O goddesses, the peace
and joy of flying fingers, the euphoria
of creation, the satisfaction of accomplishment.
Bless our tools, Frigga;
bless the hours we spend in reflection,
our minds quiet, our hands engaged
in useful work, bless us all this winter day.

Sprinkle each implement with mead from the bowl.
Sprinkle each participant with mead from the bowl.

CLOSE

To best beloved Frigga, to Saga and Eir, to Gefjon and Fulla, to Sjofn and Lofn, to Vor and Var and Syn and Hlin, to Snotra and to Gna, we offer our thanks for your many, many gifts. May the blessings of the Asynjur fall on all who have gathered here this day!

The blot is ended; may we go forth and live well, firm in our faith and strong in our bonds with our gods.

Ostara

At Ostara we honor the goddess Ostara, along with Freyja, Frey, Thor and Sif—all gods who bring the earth to life each spring, all gods we await eagerly each year. About two weeks earlier, we gather to make pysanky—Ukrainian eggs—to offer to the gods. We offer them through burial, once the ground has thawed enough to dig.

NEEDED
Mead or other beverage
Drinking horn or other vessel
Blot bowl
Eggs for offering
Eggs for blessing
Two baskets
Wildflower seeds

HALLOWING

May the hammer of Thor hallow and hold this holy place, and may Redbeard ward and watch over those gathered here today.

INTRODUCTION

In ancient times bright Ostara was a great goddess, so great that the spring season itself bore her name, and so dear to the folk that even at the height of the conversion she could never be entirely driven away.

It can be hard for us to imagine the lives of our forebears. Even those of us who live in rural areas cannot truly understand their reliance on the land, or the way their lives hinged on the turning of the seasons. When the modern small farmer or homesteader's crops fail, he has to go to the store and spend money he hadn't planned on. It might be a genuine hardship, it might only be an inconvenience, but there is food to be had. When that happened to our ancestors, they just didn't eat. And if the same bad fortune befell everyone in a community, those people were going to have a hard time of it.

At this time of year--Ostara's time--we see the very first signs of the coming spring, and although the land is still thick with snow, we know and have faith that soon it will be green again and new life will return. We understand the sense of promise and potential so precious to our ancestors, of the seed itself which, nurtured in rich soil and given sufficient rain, will one day sustain us.

Today we honor these gods without whose gifts of life and growth we could not survive: Ostara--bringer of new life whose arrival we await eagerly each year. Frey--giver of growth, whose might grants strength to crops and to beasts. Freyja--granter of lovers' wishes, provider of life and lust to all the world's creatures. Thor--master of the storm, who brings the rains of spring and summer. And to Sif--bright-haired mistress of the fields, spirit of growth and ripening.

OFFERINGS

Pour mead into horn.

Hail to Ostara, swift one, fair one.
We welcome you, we ask your blessing.
We see bare branches lined with white,
we step with care on the slick-packed snow,
waiting for the first pale leaves to sprout,
for timid crocuses to pierce the ice.
Ostara, in you we see the might
of new life, of what will be in time
and through hard work. Hail Ostara!

Pass horn, pour out remaining mead into bowl.
Place egg to be offered into offering basket.
Pour mead into horn.

Hail to Frey, kind-hearted, well-honored Van!
We welcome you, we ask your blessing.
Protector and provider of field
and farm, granter of lust and new life
to men and beasts, the cold earth herself
responds to your touch, bears fruit and grain.
Mighty Frey, stronger still in summer,
peace and pleasure and all that lives
and grows are your gifts. Hail to Frey!

Pass horn, pour out remaining mead into bowl.
Place egg to be offered into offering basket.
Pour mead into horn.

Hail to Freyja, glory of fair Asgard!
We welcome you, we ask your blessing.
Bearer of peerless Brisingamen,
embodiment of unknowable might;
you know of those things that drive us most,
the desires that compel our survival.
Wise and willful Freyja, driver of cats,
mistress of far-famed Folkvang, granter of
our most heartfelt wishes. Hail to Freyja!

Pass horn, pour out remaining mead into bowl.
Place egg to be offered into offering basket.
Pour mead into horn.

Hail to Thor, red-bearded son of Odin!
We welcome you, we ask your blessing.
Slayer of giants, the foes of Asgard,
friend of the men and women of Midgard,
upholder of the order of the world,
wielder of the thunderbolt, bearer
of matchless Mjollnir, master of the warm
spring rains that bring the deep-sunk seeds to life,
master of the lightning. Hail to Thor!

Pass horn, pour out remaining mead into bowl.
Place egg to be offered into offering basket. Pour mead into horn.

Hail to Sif of the yellow hair, whose will
it is that brings the fruited field to life
and to completion. Glorious bride of Thor,
fair flower of Asgard, treasure of the gods,
goddess unsurpassed in all the worlds,
in kindness and in goodness, in beauty
and in might. Sif of the rowan-tree,
Sif of the golden sheaf, Sif whose hand
we see in the earth's return. Hail to Sif!

Pass horn, pour out remaining mead into bowl.
Place egg to be offered into offering basket.

EGG BLESSING

Some of you have also brought eggs to have blessed, and to bring home with
you; if you'd like and are comfortable doing so, please feel free to share
anything you'd like to about them.

Fair Ostara, giver of new life and new strength, we ask your blessing on these
eggs, that they may bring health, vitality, and good fortune throughout the
year to come.

***Each person passes their egg around the circle, placing it in the
blessing basket.***

Sprinkle each implement with mead from the bowl.
Sprinkle each participant with mead from the bowl.

SEED BLESSING

To mark Ostara's season, as well as our bonds as a kindred, we want
everyone to take home some of these wildflower seeds, to plant at home as
you see fit, as a reminder of Ostara's might and of the bonds we share and
have shared as a group over the past years.

Ostara, whose hand we see in each new blade of grass, each budding leaf on
bare tree limbs, we thank you for your many gifts, and we ask your blessing
on these seeds, that they may flourish in the earth we live on.

Each person takes some seeds.

CLOSE

To long-awaited Ostara, mighty Frey and glorious Freyja, to friend Thor and golden Sif: we give our thanks for your blessings, both in the past and still to come. May you bless all who have gathered here today.

The blot is ended; may we go forth and live well, firm in our faith and strong in our bonds with our gods.

May Day

May Day is Freyja's day. Even though we have had more than one May Day interrupted by snow or freezing temperatures, it is still Freyja's Day, the day we celebrate all the joy and pleasure she brings to us.

NEEDED
Mead or other beverage
Drinking horn or other vessel
Blot bowl

HALLOWING

May the hammer of Thor hallow and hold this place, and may Redbeard ward and watch over those gathered here today.

INTRODUCTION

It is said, and it is so, that in spring the minds of men and women turn to thoughts of love. The warm sun on our skin, the feel of moist earth in our hands, the sharp spring winds tossing our hair--all these bring to mind the many pleasures of the flesh, and that most wonderful and beautiful of goddesses whose might touches each one of us at our core: Freyja!

READING

One day on her travels Freyja journeyed deep within the earth, to the halls of the dwarves. Now, the dwarves are the finest craftsmen in all the worlds, and many are the treasures of dwarven art held by the gods--the irresistable hammer of Thor, the flawless ship of Frey, the abundant golden hair of Sif. And so when Freyja saw the necklace Brisingamen--a prize as rare, as beautiful, as mighty as any ever forged--she knew she had to possess it and was well prepared to pay any price to gain it. She offered the dwarven smiths great riches, but so precious was Brisingamen, so loathe were its creators to suffer its loss, that they would consider no payment in earthly gold or jewels.

158

No, the only payment they would accept, the only treasure that would repay them for the forfeit of Brisingamen, must come from the goddess herself. One night in turn must Freyja spend with each dwarven craftsman, and then would the brilliant necklace be hers. A sacrifice, yes, but an inevitable one once she had seen the gem. Freyja paid the fee, freely and willingly. The dwarves had their reward, and she held the inestimable Brisingamen, to wear and to wield as she willed.

INVITATION

Freya, we know you as a wise and glorious goddess, as a sorceress of unparallelled might and finesse, and as a skilled player at games of war and love. Today we honor you, Freyja; we thank you for your many gifts, we ask your blessing on those gathered here today.

OFFERINGS

Pour mead into horn.

Hail to Freyja, brightest bloom of Asgard,
great and mighty goddess, essence of passion.
Freyja, driver of cats, whose steady hand
guides us with subtlety and certainty;
Freyja, seeker of might and wisdom,
who teaches us to understand the cost
of what we desire; Freyja, granter of joy
and pleasure, who inspires us to relish
the gifts of the earth. Freyja, shining one,
who holds us in her arms, who sharpens our wits,
who for a precious moment lets us see
through her eyes the wonders of the worlds.
Freyja, daughter of the worthy Vans,
holder of mysteries, holder of wisdom,
holder of the brilliant Brisingamen,
we praise and honor you this day. Hail Freyja!

Pass horn, pour out remaining mead into bowl.

CLOSE

To Freyja, fair lady of the Vans, we give our thanks for your blessings, both in the past and still to come. May you bless all who have gathered here today.

The blot is ended; may we go forth and live well, firm in our faith and strong in our bonds with our gods.

Midsummer

At Midsummer we honor a wide selection of gods. The ritual script allows for the inclusion of nineteen—you can omit some or add more, as you prefer. A warning: make sure everyone knows how many rounds there will be, so they can adjust their drinking accordingly (taking small sips, for example) if the drink is alcoholic.

NEEDED
Mead or other beverage
Drinking horn or other vessel
Blot bowl

HALLOWING

May the hammer of Thor hallow and hold this place, and may Redbeard ward and watch over those gathered here today.

INTRODUCTION

Midsummer is a time of gathering. All around the world, people enjoy the longer days and come together for feasts and festivals. In older times the Thing--the annual assembly of the people of the community--was held at this time. Today we, too, make use of the fair weather and travel near and far to join with friends and family. Because together we are stronger, wiser, happier than we are alone. Together we can accomplish much. Together we can better our lives and our world. With frith and friendship, we can build our community, strengthen our bonds with the gods and with each other.

The gods, too, gather together often, for strength and for companionship; the gods, too, take joy in fellowship:

At Ithavoll met the mighty gods,
Shrines and temples they timbered high;
Forges they set, and they smithied ore,
Tongs they wrought, and tools they fashioned.

In their dwellings at peace they played at tables,
Of gold no lack did the gods then know.
(Voluspa 7-8)

At Midsummer, we gather together, and we consider the many gifts given us by the gods. Because, whether or not we are aware of it, each god touches us, each affects our lives, each is due our thanks. At Midsummer, we **are** mindful of this. We honor the gods, one by one, and we think about what they mean to us--what they mean to the world.

INVITATION

Hail the Aesir! Hail the Vanir!
For all you are we praise you;
For all good things we thank you.
On this holy tide,
in this holy stead,
we honor you, gods and goddesses.

OFFERINGS

Pour mead into horn.

Hail to Odin, Allfather, breath-giver,
seeker of wisdom, seizer of knowledge,
a gift for a gift, value for value,
pain for insight, all you know well.
The sons and daughters of ash and elm
call to you, wise one of many names.
We give you thanks for our own might,
we give you thanks for the gift of will,
for choices offered, for the long view taken.
Hail to Odin! Hail the wanderer!

Pass horn, pour out remaining mead into bowl. Pour mead into horn.

Hail to Frigga, wise and knowing goddess,
great lady of Asgard, mistress of Fensalir,
whose guiding hand pulls order from chaos,
whose keen eye sees the patterns of existence,
whose presence makes our footing firm.
Beloved Frigga, fair one, judicious one,
wary and watchful, perceptive and aware,
guardian of children, defender of family,
holder of harmony, heart of the home,
we thank you for your blessings. Hail Frigga!

Pass horn, pour out remaining mead into bowl. Pour mead into horn.

Hail to red Thor, champion of Asgard,
wielder of Mjolnir, slayer of giants,
defender against the foes of order.
For bringing the rains, for warding the worlds,
for preserving the bounds, we thank you.
Thor, friend of man, defender of travelers,
son of crafty Odin and life-giving Jord,
husband of Sif of the golden hair,
father of those who will endure the end,
we honor you and all your deeds. Hail Thor!

Pass horn, pour out remaining mead into bowl.
Pour mead into horn.

Hail to Sif, shining light of fair Asgard,
whose soft voice speaks words of wisdom and might,
whose gentle touch guides subtly but firmly,
whose hair of true gold shines like the sun.
Incomparable Sif, bride of red Thor,
whose hands hold the heart of the thunderer,
mother of children both comely and strong,
compassionate goddess, who holds each child
within her arms, who shows us the substance
within our souls. Hail Sif, steadfast goddess!

Pass horn, pour out remaining mead into bowl.
Pour mead into horn.

Hail to fair Frey, lord of verdant Alfheim;
son of noble Njord, most mighty of Vans;
suitor, then husband, of the peerless Gerd,
for whom your passion, headstrong and abiding,
drove from you all sense--your love for the maid
transcended reason, transcended duty,
as the call of life transcends the fear of death.
Holder of the seed, digger in the dirt,
god whose might draws each green shoot from the soil
and sparks desire in man and beast--Hail Frey!

***Pass horn, pour out remaining mead into bowl.
Pour mead into horn.***

Hail to bright Freyja, hail the Vanadis,
hail, goddess whose wisdom, might and agile wit
work wonders in the worlds. Hail Freyja,
whose steady hand makes sure the most headstrong
of beasts, whose radiance and grace make silent
the most eloquent of men. Hail Freyja,
whose voice we hear in the words of lovers,
whose heartbeat we feel in the throes of desire.
Freyja, shining Freyja, amber-teared goddess
who of love and pain knows all. Hail Freyja!

***Pass horn, pour out remaining mead into bowl.
Pour mead into horn.***

Hail to UllR, hail the god of the hunt!
Hail UllR, whose aim is ever true,
whose arm is strong, whose eye is keen,
whose step is sure in deep-drifted snow
or on treacherous ice, who roams the woods,
who knows each tree, each nest, each hiding place,
who knows the ways of every beast. UllR,
son of bright-haired Sif, bowman unsurpassed,
unyielding one who travels, free and fleet,
through winter's rage. Hail UllR! Hail the bow-god!

Pass horn, pour out remaining mead into bowl. Pour mead into horn.

Hail Skadhi, keen-witted daughter of Thiazi!
Steel-eyed goddess, fair-browed etin-bride,
bow-woman who strikes swiftly, surely,
with power and precision. Mountain-woman,
friend of wolves, whose distant howls bring comfort
and solace, who joined with the Aesir
not from need but from desire, for always
could bright Skadhi stand alone and prevail.
Peerless woman, strong of bow-arm, swift of shaft,
of worth and honor you know much. Hail Skadhi!

Pass horn, pour out remaining mead into bowl.
Pour mead into horn.

Hail to Njord, elder Van who came to Asgard
long ago, when blood lay warm on the field
of battle, when As and Van matched might and wit,
each finding in the foe an equal and a friend.
Njord, bringer of peace, giver of wealth,
ally of merchants, fair-footed sea-god,
distant love of shining Skadhi, a match
unsuited, a heart held ever close;
Njord, who we know as we walk on the shore,
standing at once in sand and sea. Hail Njord!

Pass horn, pour out remaining mead into bowl.
Pour mead into horn.

Hail to Nerthus, ancient and wondrous,
hidden goddess who holds her secrets close,
peace-bringing goddess whose presence forbids
quarrels and conflicts, and all devices
of war. Deep-rooted Nerthus, Vanic mother,
of your shroud and wain we know little;
of your hand in the world we see much,
but our grasp of your might is feeble.
Hail to Nerthus, who knows of seed and soil,
who sees beneath all cloaks and masks. Hail Nerthus!

Pass horn, pour out remaining mead into bowl. Pour mead into horn.

Hail to one-armed Tyr, just one, noble one.
Hail Tyr, whose oldest tales remain untold;
hail Tyr, whose deepest roots remain undug.
A friend to the wolf you once were, O Tyr;
when called to serve both honor and need,
you chose the path of pain and loss, your hand
was taken--your word you kept. Tyr, who we
call on for justice, whose gifts are given
with an even hand, who knows which man
bears guilt and which is honest. Hail to Tyr!

***Pass horn, pour out remaining mead into bowl.
Pour mead into horn.***

Hail to bright Heimdall, keen-eyed watcher
over Bifrost, bearer of the Gjallarhorn,
keeper of the gate, holder of the bridge,
first defender of peerless Asgard.
Heimdall, who hears the leaves fall from the trees
and the blades of grass pierce the rich soil,
honored father of men, shaper of mankind,
giver of magic, teacher of rune-craft,
fair-faced As, child of the nine mothers,
elder god, ancient one. Hail to Heimdall!

***Pass horn, pour out remaining mead into bowl.
Pour mead into horn.***

Hail to Forseti, son of bright Balder
and kind-hearted Nanna, master of Glitnir,
wise one whose level head and even hand
bring peace to those driven by quarrels
and feuds, whose certain sense of the just
and the fair resolves all disputes.
Yours is the best of courts, Forseti,
god of the pure spring, god of the swift tongue,
sense-speaking god who brought the law to men,
strife-stiller, frith-bringer. Hail Forseti!

Pass horn, pour out remaining mead into bowl. Pour mead into horn.

Hail to Bragi, wise one, long-bearded one,
word-weaver, tale-spinner, best of bards,
most skillful of skalds. Bragi, learned one,
rune-tongued master of stories and songs,
a merry tale can you tell in a trice,
or one to bring quick tears to all eyes.
With sweetened words you make welcome the guest,
with nimble wit you shift the minds of men.
Bragi, whose spark we seek, whose fire we crave,
whose touch we know but rarely. Hail Bragi!

***Pass horn, pour out remaining mead into bowl.
Pour mead into horn.***

Hail to Idunna, bright bloom of Asgard,
beloved wife of long-bearded Bragi,
watchful guardian of the sweet apples
of youth and vigor. Fair Idunna,
stolen by greedy Thiazi you were,
but by Loki's wit and Freyja's cloak
you were returned, holding close the treasured fruit.
Idunna, who knows when to speak in company
and when to keep silent, whose lightest touch
cheers the heart and lightens the step. Hail Idunna!

***Pass horn, pour out remaining mead into bowl.
Pour mead into horn.***

Hail to Balder, Odin-son, best and brightest,
much-loved god whose fair fame and good repute
only reflect a kind heart, a true mettle,
an honor unblemished, a worth unsurpassed.
Master of Breidablik, most splended of halls;
son of fair Frigga, husband of Nanna.
In dreams you saw your end and the worlds';
brave Balder, honored guest in Helheim's depths,
patiently you wait for the far-away day
of your return, of the worlds' rebirth. Hail Balder!

Pass horn, pour out remaining mead into bowl. Pour mead into horn.

Hail to fair Nanna, daughter of Nepr,
wife of bright Balder, devoted and true,
mother of silken-tongued Forseti.
Might-giving goddess, intrepid and bold,
fearless and faithful, you followed your love
on his most daunting journey, to share
his fate and his life, wherever they lead,
to burn with him on the crested sea,
to dwell with him in the halls of Hella,
to rise with him at the end of all things.

***Pass horn, pour out remaining mead into bowl.
Pour mead into horn.***

Hail to merry Aegir, best of brewers
whose ale and mead flows ever freely,
whose open hand and hearty good cheer
make welcome the guest and the traveler.
In your gold-lit hall the gods take their ease,
as the fine ale pours itself into each horn.
Aegir, the dark depths of the sea are yours,
and the wild waves frothing far above,
your nine fair daughters, each a treasure,
each a sailor's dream. Hail to Aegir!

***Pass horn, pour out remaining mead into bowl.
Pour mead into horn.***

Hail to Ran, fair bride of noble Aegir,
who holds the keys to the finest of halls,
who guides the drowned man to his final rest,
with a seat by the hearth and a horn of good ale,
to feast and tell tales far beneath the storm.
Ran, whose well-knotted net is ever ready,
whose nine daughters roam the oceans at will,
stirrer of seas, stealer of souls,
in the rush of waves we hear your voice,
in the sharp salt spray we feel your touch.

Pass horn, pour out remaining mead into bowl.

CLOSE

To god and goddess, As and Van, we thank you for your presence.

The blot is ended; may we go forth and live well, firm in our faith and strong in our bonds with our gods.

Freyfaxi

At Freyfaxi we honor not only Frey, but all the Vanir in what is, at its heart, their season. Freyja, Frey, Nerthus and Njord, all receive our thanks for their many blessings.

NEEDED
Mead or other beverage
Drinking horn or other vessel
Blot bowl

HALLOWING

May the hammer of Thor hallow and hold this holy place, and my Redbeard ward and watch over those gathered here today.

INTRODUCTION

Here we have a quick summer season, only a brief time to warm our bones in the hot sun, only a few short months to grow and gather winter stores. In this we take joy. We savor these days as we savor the taste of fruit from the tree; we drink them in as we drink the sweet mead we share with the gods. In this season, we feel more than ever the might of the Vans.

Hail to the Vans! Knowing ones, ancient ones, mighty ones
who in elder times broke down the walls of Asgard,
who trampled and tore the very field of battle,
who found in the noble Aesir an even match,
a wise accord, a balanced realm of friend and peer.
From Vanaheim your line arose--fair Vanaheim,
land of green mead and quiet wood, of waters deep
and barrows long enclosed. To bright-halled Asgard
came you four--Nerthus and Njord, Freyja and Frey--
to join your might with the fair Aesir, to share
with them your knowledge and your wisdom, to bring
to that land a lusty nature and a merry heart.

Farsighted gods of the Vanir, we thank you for
the roots that dig into the earth, for the black soil
beneath our feet and the seed that lies so deep within,
for the food we eat, for the daughters and sons
who bring joy to our lives and strength to our kin,
for each and every beat of our heart--for all this,
dear Vanir, we thank you. Hail the gods who bring life
to our lives! Hail the gods of shining Vanaheim!

OFFERINGS

Pour mead into horn.

Hail Frey, lord of the fields we sow and reap,
lord of the beasts whose lives sustain our own,
lord of the light-elves, of the green meads
and wildwoods of Alfheim, yours as a tooth-gift.
We thank you for the gifts of the earth,
who cares for us as we care for her.
We thank you for the needs of the body,
the cravings that drive us ever toward life.
Hail to Frey, granter of good, fair-faced Van
whose hand we see in the growing world.

Pass horn, pour out remaining mead into bowl.
Pour mead into horn.

Hail Freyja, peerless goddess, honey-tongued one
whose persuasion and guile can charm all the world,
fair one whose soft voice hides an iron will
and a resolute heart. Freyja, whose hold
on the souls of men is firm, whose might
and wit are unrivaled in all of Asgard,
who knows the heat of desire and the chill
of love lost, we thank you for the sweetest
moments of life, for the passions that bring us
out of ourselves and into the divine.

Pass horn, pour out remaining mead into bowl.
Pour mead into horn.

Hail to Njord, fair-footed lord of Noatun,
god of the seacoasts, of well-traveled paths
and of routes uncharted, of journeys unknown,
of merchants and traders, farmers and fishers,
of the wealth of the world in land and in gold.
Njord, who sees what is through Vanic eyes,
who we find where the sand meets the sea,
who carries the might of soil and stone,
whose good humor and openhandedness
are unmatched in all the worlds. Hail to Njord!

***Pass horn, pour out remaining mead into bowl.
Pour mead into horn.***

Hail to Nerthus, deep-rooted goddess,
heart of the Vanir, soul of the earth,
center and source of our existence.
Straight and true your wagon fared, Nerthus,
drawn by kind-eyed cows, veiled in fine cloth,
served by doomed men, your secrets still unknown.
Nerthus, ancient one, knowing one, mother of gods,
within the blood and bone of old Ymir
you dwell, from icy peaks to fiery depths.
Field and furrow, seed and soil, all are yours.

Pass horn, pour out remaining mead into bowl.

CLOSE

To all the ancient, noble Vans, to Frey and Freyja, Njord and Nerthus, we give our thanks for all you have granted us. May you bless all who have gathered here today.

The blot is ended; may we go forth and live well, firm in our faith and strong in our bonds with our gods.

Winter Finding

By the Autumn Equinox, we generally have little trouble with Winter Finding—it is easily found, and in some years we have celebrated it with fresh-fallen snow on the ground! We mark the occasion by welcoming two gods we know very, very well—Skadhi and UllR!

Needed

Mead or other beverage
Drinking horn or other vessel
Blot bowl
Hunting implements for blessing

HALLOWING

May the hammer of Thor hallow and hold this place, and may Redbeard ward and watch over those gathered here today.

INTRODUCTION

Summer has come and gone, my friends, and with it
the long days, the sun beating down, the green-clad trees.
Harvest too has passed us now; the food we gathered
lies in our larders, jelly jars lined up like jewels
on a crown. Winter waits, just over the hill;
we see it in the early morning, the pale grass
crisped by early frosts. We hear it in the cries
of birds as they make their way to warmer climes.
We feel it in our bones, we know it in our hearts,
for we are Winter's folk, the folk of shining Skadhi,
the folk of brave UllR, the folk of the north.

INVITATION

Today we call to UllR and to Skadhi, who come to us each year at this time. This is your season, kindly ones, your world of ice and snow, and we who live in it do so by your good will. Skadhi! UllR! We thank you for your many gifts, the many boons you have granted us. We ask your blessings on those gathered here today.

OFFERINGS

Pour mead into horn.

Bright-eyed Skadhi, daughter of the mountain-giant,
child of the snow and ice, wood-roaming goddess,
firm of footing, firm of purpose, firm of will.
We welcome you, we welcome your strength, we welcome
your season. Skadhi of the cold, shrill winds, the darkened
skies, the frozen earth, Skadhi of sharpened shafts
and feathered flights, stout-armed bow-woman, sure
of hand and sturdy of heart. Grant to us a keen eye
and a steady hand, grant to us full freezers
and safe journeys. Hail to Skadhi! Hail winter's maid!

Pass horn, pour out remaining mead into bowl.
Pour mead into horn.

UllR of the northern lands, UllR of the cold
and the stinging wind, bow-god, hunting-god,
deer-stalker, sharp-eyed tracker of bird and beast.
We welcome you, we welcome your strength, we welcome
your season. UllR, glory of the gods, bearer
of the oathring, master of bright-halled Ydalir
that stands among the green-boughed yew, rune-master,
son of Sif, elf-friend, wise and prudent chief. Grant us skill
and silence as we step on crusted snow, grant to us
a season safe from harm. Hail to lordly UllR!

Pass horn, pour out remaining mead into bowl.

HUNTER BLESSING

Anyone who has brought a hunting implement may place it on the altar.

Hail to UllR and to Skadhi, gods whose share
of the year we we welcome each autumn, for each
share has its fortunes and its perils. Gods
of the cold, gods of the hunt, gods who guide us
through the long winter, we ask your blessing.
May our arm be steady, may our aim be true,
grant us a safe and successful hunting season.
May our footing be firm, may our path never swerve,
as we make our way along ice or through storms.

Sprinkle each implement with mead from the bowl.
Sprinkle each participant with mead from the bowl.

CLOSE

To UllR and to Skadhi, we give our thanks for blessings received and still to come. May your blessings fall on all who have gathered here this day!

The blot is ended; may we go forth and live well, firm in our faith and strong in our bonds with our gods.

Winternights

On Winternights we honor those who have gone before us, those who have passed on into Hella's realm, our Disir and Alfar, and those whose lives have inspired our own.

NEEDED
Mead or other beverage
Drinking horn or other vessel
Blot bowl
Tea lights
Lit candle

HALLOWING

May the hammer of Thor hallow and hold this place, and may Redbeard ward and watch over those gathered here today.

INTRODUCTION

At Winternights, as the days grow cold and the nights
grow long, we gather together to think of those
who are no longer in our lives, and of the fair one
in whose household those long-lost loved ones now dwell.
We pass the horn and share our memories of those dear
to us, those whose might still resonates in our world,
those whose names we bear, those whose luck we share,
those who one day we will join in the halls of Hella,
and what a merry, joyful union that will be!

OFFERINGS

Pour mead into horn.

Gracious Hella, noble lady of the afterworld,
defender of bright Balder, kind-hearted guardian
of those who have entered your realm. Child of chaos,
keeper of order, mistress of the roomy halls
of shining Helheim, guardian of the frigid plains
of Niflhel, your gate held firm against all ill.
To our beloved dead you show your face so fair;
your fearsome visage you reserve for those whose evil
carries them to Nastrond's shore. Hella, best of hosts,
open-handed receiver of guests, your hearth
and your table you share with those who have passed
into your domain. Hail to Hella, hail the holder
of hope! We thank you for the blessings you grant to those
we have loved in this world, we thank you for a welcome
still to come. Hail to Hella, hail your safe haven!

Pass horn, pour out remaining mead into bowl.
Pour mead into horn.

Beloved ones, friends and kin long gone, family lost
to time and distance, grandmothers and grandfathers
of centuries past, you whose loss still cuts knife-sharp
and you we know only from oft-repeated tales.
Honored ones, you whose lives inspire us, you whose deeds
shaped history for good or ill, whose blood runs through our veins,
you whose bold and restless hearts brought us to new lands,
you to whom we owe our lives and our existence,
we remember you this night. We see your faces
in the mirror each day, we see your spirit
in our children's eyes. We see the world we live in
and recognize your hand in it; we find our way
through life and know your lives as well. Through the years
we hear your voice, we feel your gaze, we know your love
and care. Hail to the dead, hail to our foundation.

Pass horn, pour out remaining mead into bowl.

REMEMBRANCE

At this point we honor the dead as individuals. Each person in turn takes a tealight and lights it on the main candle, saying something about the person they are remembering and putting the lit tealight on the table. After each remembrance, all present say "We remember." This can be done for a predetermined number of rounds or until everyone has finished, depending on the size of the group.

CLOSE

To kind Hella and to all the honored dead, we thank you for what you have given us, and we ask your blessings in years to come.

The blot is ended; may we go forth and live well, firm in our faith and strong in our bonds with our gods.

Home Blessing

This ritual is to be done upon moving into a new house. There are really two parts to it; in the first part, all present walk the perimeter of the property, led by the homeowner(s), who carry the lantern or candle (taking care that the flame doesn't go out). This may not always be possible, as in the case of an apartment or condominium In other cases—if the property is very large, for example—the owner(s) may wish to do this beforehand, on their own. When we did it, we walked once around the yard surrounding our house, starting and ending at the front door, at which point I drew an Othala rune on the front door and continued the rest of the ritual as written.

The "heart of the home" is whatever central spot you feel the most comfortable, perhaps the kitchen or living room.

NEEDED
Candle or lantern (for walking the perimeter)
Mead or other beverage
Drinking horn or other vessel
Blot bowl

Stand at the front door.

HALLOWING

May the hammer of Thor hallow and hold this place, and may Redbeard ward and watch over those gathered here today.

Open the door, but don't cross the threshold yet.

THRESHOLD PRAYER

Hail to Frigga, Beloved, holder of the home.
As we cross this threshold we enter your domain,
you whose firm hand we feel guiding us through each day,
whose keen mind we -- as we plan our lives,
whose sharp gaze we follow as we watch our children,
whose warm heart we know as we join with friends and family.

Cross the threshold.
Move to the heart of the home.

WELCOMING

As our household moves into this, our new home, we welcome the gods.

Pour mead into horn.

Odin, Allfather, seeker of knowledge,
builder of intricacies, we make you welcome.

Frigga, kind one, sharp-witted wise woman,
supporter of families, we make you welcome.

Thor, Redbeard, strong-armed wielder of Mjolnir,
guardian of mankind, we make you welcome.

Golden-tressed Sif, bright light of fair Asgard,
gentle-handed one, we make you welcome.

Frey, fair Vanic lord, rooted in the deep earth,
pure green flame of life, we make you welcome.

Freyja, skilled driver of cats, wielder of
Brisingamen's might, we make you welcome.

Tyr, one-handed warrior, foe of chaos
who does what must be done, we make you welcome.

Heimdall, guardian of many-colored Bifrost,
granter of knowledge, we make you welcome.

Skadhi, sharp-witted mistress of snow and ice,
daughter of Thiazi, we make you welcome.

UllR, snowshoe god, forest-dwelling one,
patron of hunters, we make you welcome.

Forseti, fair arbiter, bringer of frith,
and balanced judgment, we make you welcome.

Nerthus, soul of the soil on which we walk,
great mother of Vans, we make you welcome.

Njord, kind-hearted granter of wealth and of weal,
white-footed sea god, we make you welcome.

Aegir, finest and most generous of hosts,
brewer of fine ale, we make you welcome.

Pass horn, pour out remaining mead into bowl

CLOSE

To all the gods and goddesses, be ever welcome in our home.

The blot is ended; may we go forth and live well, firm in our faith and strong
in our bonds with our gods.

Rite to Ran for One Who Has Drowned

NEEDED
Mead or other beverage
Drinking horn or other vessel
Offering of gold

HALLOWING

May the hammer of Thor hallow and hold this place, and may Redbeard ward and watch over those gathered here today.

INTRODUCTION

In times past, the goddess Ran, wife of the sea-god Aegir, was known to men as both fair and fearsome. Her hand was seen in shipwrecks; her name was spoken in quiet tones when a man never returned from a long sea voyage. Those who died by drowning could expect to find themselves in her house, enjoying a warm welcome in her excellent company. The wise and reverent sailor would make sure to carry with him a bit of gold, to give the noble goddess in return for her hospitality--a shining guest-gift for the beautiful Ran.

INVITATION

Pour mead into horn.

Awesome Ran, bride of Aegir, breathtaking goddess,
mistress of the white-capped waves, of the black sea-depths,
lady of the gold-lit halls, I call to you.
Gracious Ran, with open arms you welcome the dead,
those souls whose lives were lost at sea, whose last long breath
of freezing brine carried them to your shining realm.
Kind-hearted one, receiver of all who sink beneath
the seafoam, within your hall dwells one I know.

The horn is passed, and any who want to can say what they wish of the deceased, speaking of their worth and why they would be fit to spend the afterlife in Ran's hall.

Pour the mead into the sea.

OFFERING

Hold up the offering.

Glorious Ran, noble one, cupbearer to the gods,
whose hall is ever merry and warm, whose table
holds bread and meat enough to feed all who come,
whose mead is honey-sweet and smooth as sea-swept stone,
I ask of you, make welcome our dear _____,
who made his way from our world into yours. Goddess,
accept this gift of shining gold, as gift for gift
is our way and yours. Grant him your kindness and good cheer.

Drop or throw the offering into the sea.

CLOSE

Ran of the stormclouds, Ran of the churning seas, we thank you for blessings granted, we thank you for kindness shown, to our comrade _____ and to our elder kin.

The blot is ended; may we go forth and live well, firm in our faith and strong in our bonds with our gods.

Lightning Source UK Ltd.
Milton Keynes UK
UKOW04f1832211115

263244UK00001B/73/P